BECOMING

A Spiritual Guide for Navigating Adulthood

Kayla Parker

Editor

Skinner House Books

Boston

www.skinnerhouse.org

Printed in the United States

Cover design by Suzanne Morgan
Text design by Jeff Miller

print ISBN: 978-1-55896-745-8
eBook ISBN: 978-1-55896-746-5

7 6 5 4
21 20

Library of Congress Cataloging-in-Publication Data

Becoming : a spiritual guide for navigating adulthood / Kayla Parker, editor.
    pages cm
  ISBN 978-1-55896-745-8 (pbk. : alk. paper)—ISBN 978-1-55896-746-5
(ebook) 1. Meditations. 2. Unitarian Universalist Association. 3. Young
adults—Religious life. I. Parker, Kayla.
  BX9855.B43 2014
  248.8'4—dc23

2014018259

Every effort has been made to obtain permission for each of these pieces. In some
cases the author is deceased and we have been unable to locate their estate. Credit
lines appear on pages 152–64 and 169.

Contents

Special thanks to John F. and Susan B. Smith,
whose leadership, generosity, and commitment to
UU young adult spirituality and service
helped to make this book possible.

Preface

Who are young adults, really? We can define ourselves by the number of years we have spent on this earth and, more importantly, by the fact that we are constantly in transition, constantly becoming. This state of perpetual change has become our internal metronome; we ignore, resist, and struggle to keep up with its rhythm, or we accept and improvise along with it. Ideally we stay with the beat, but we are only human and sometimes we simply cannot keep up. The tempo can be so much faster, slower, or just plain different than what we have known before.

I suspect that constant change is something people of all ages contend with—and that the readings in this book might strike a chord with people of many generations. This book is for young adults—and all who are forever becoming. However many years you have moved about this earth, I hope these words will accompany you on your journey. May they help you reflect, be present in the moment, and look toward the future.

This little book is organized into themes relevant to the lives of young adults and seeks to give voice to a variety of opinions and experiences on these topics. Each thematic section includes three types of readings: opening and closing words (two of each), reflections (two), and poems and prayers (eight).

The opening and closing words might be used as prayers or meditations for individuals or groups. They can easily become rising and bedtime meditations for a person or family, or readings to begin and end a small group meeting or worship. The reflections are the soul of this collection, and come from Unitarian Universalist young adults based on their own lives and learnings. Finally, the poems and prayers are compiled from a wide variety of sources, from ancient Sufi texts to current Unitarian Universalist leaders. The reflections, as well as the prayers and poems, might be used for personal contemplation, small group conversations, or as liturgical elements in worship.

I hope that the writings in this book will speak to you and become your companions in this unpredictable life. May they speak to your heart and soul, and move with you throughout your days.

Every word in these pages was written or chosen by people who want you to know that you are not alone—we are all becoming. We wrote, compiled, and edited not only to share our own truths, but to be next to you as you discover yours.

In communion, solidarity, and love,

Kayla

Growth and Change

OPENING WORDS

We do not grow absolutely, chronologically. We grow sometimes in one dimension, and not in another, unevenly. We grow partially. We are relative. We are mature in one realm, childish in another. The past, present, and future mingle and pull us backward, forward, or fix us in the present. We are made of layers, cells, constellations.

—*Anaïs Nin*

No summer ever came back, and no two summers ever were alike. Times change, and people change; and if our hearts do not change as readily, so much the worse for us.

—*Nathaniel Hawthorne*

REFLECTION

Trust Walk

My high school years were speckled with trust walks. In my Unitarian Universalist youth group at the First UU Congregation of Ann Arbor, each year, the incoming freshmen were given blindfolds and a partner. They were led out into the dark, with only hands on their shoulders to guide them. When it was my turn to be blindfolded, I found, while stumbling over gravel in the parking lot and trudging up the hills behind my church, that despite all the efforts to fool me, the whole time I knew exactly where I was. This was ground I knew. Before even pressing down my foot I knew exactly how much the earth would give beneath me. I knew I was safe. I trusted the people around me, but it was easy. I knew I could have gotten along without them.

After high school I moved away for college and was looking for the belonging that I had found at home. I joined a poetry group, and our first meeting included an initiation ceremony that reminded me of my youth group trust walks. The evening started with a scavenger hunt around town and culminated in a trust walk. Blindfolded by the more senior members, I could not orient myself in the dark. For the first time in my life, I was truly lost. In this new town, I barely knew where I was with my eyes open. When I allowed a new acquaintance to guide me, I truly gave them control.

Growing up, I was fortunate to be able to find ground I loved and people I connected to at church. When I moved, the trauma of leaving such a beautiful home led me to be incredibly insecure my first few weeks away. Once, when I introduced myself, the person I was meeting told me, "You say 'Ann Arbor' like it's the center of the universe." To me, it was. It was how I related myself to the world. It was where my friends lived. I believed I could not love the people in my new home in the same way. They hadn't watched me stumble through adolescence; they would never really know me. I felt that I was living away from where my life truly was.

I only started to adjust when the fall colors began to paint the trees around me. I found a sense of familiarity in the season. Time had not stopped even though little else in life felt continuous.

When I took a second to fall in love with fall, I started taking time to fall in love with the people around me. I began to discover the ways in which my new friends were similar to my other friends, and to appreciate the ways in which they were different. I learned to be comfortable with not always recognizing the similarities.

People keep telling me that in order to make the most of this time, I must live like I am dying. I find this idea constricting because so much of the idea of dying for me involves being my final, complete self—the person I want to grow into. This self, who lives her values perfectly and only creates beauty, is quite far away from who I am now. Instead of trying to achieve that impossible state, I am letting go for now. By allowing myself to trust the future and the change that comes with it, I get to stop and question. I do not need to rush.

Today I'm with new people, learning new norms, and new definitions of everything I thought I understood. I'm learning to take steps forward, without knowing whether the ground will hold me. I do not look down to search for familiarity, but instead look forward to the seasons ahead, to the inevitable change and growth.

—*Rianna Johnson-Levy*

POEMS AND PRAYERS

Some Day

Once upon a time I was
Now I am
Some day I will become

Once there was
And now there is
Soon there will be
And some day there surely shall be

Once upon a time we were
Now we are
And some day (Hallelujah!) we shall surely become

Amen
Amen

—*Margaret Williams Braxton*

I Say It Touches Us

I say that it touches us that our blood is
    sea water and our tears are salt, that the
    seed of our bodies is scarcely different
    from the same cells in a seaweed,
    and that the stuff of our bones is like the coral.

I say that the tide rolls in on us, whether
    we like it or not, and the sands of time
    keep running their intended course.

I say we have to go down into the wave's trough
    to find ourselves, and then ride her swell
    until we can see beyond ourselves into
    our neighbor's eye.

I say that we shall never leave the harbor
    if we do not hoist the sail.

I say that we have got to walk the waves
    as well as solid ground.

I say that anyone who goes without
    consciousness of this will remain
    chained to a rusty anchor.

May the journey find us worthy. Amen.

—Marni P. Harmony

This Body

This body is not what it was
I got shin splints from running today
    Ten years ago all I'd get was smelly feet
My back aches just from sitting these days
    In my youth, all my pain came from climbing trees

This body is not what it was
Not some alien thing thrust upon me
    So clumsy, always in the way
I know it and move it like it's mine
    Didn't say I never walk into walls from time to time

This body is not what it will be
When the sagging of old age sets in
    And simple backaches are fond memories
So I'll take and enjoy what it is right now
    Not yet frail from old age but sometimes awkward and weak
(Really, it suits what's inside quite nicely)

This body is not what it was
Or what it will be
And thankfully, right now
It seems to just fit me

—Kayla Parker

Lucky Streak

Who cast a spell over my world?
Who opened the doors,
stirred the crowd of possibilities,
put gold dust in my dreams
causing my life to turn?

O Fate, O Love, O Spirit, O God:
is it true
that all good things must end?

Or have you set me on a path of meaning
    Not luck
Of clarity
    Not magic

And this grace
that brought me to the mountaintop
is also assigned to carry me through dark forests of
    loss,
        the ones that await us all,
        that disturb our peaceful sleep.

The same grace that guides the seasons:
cracking the ice,
pushing up saplings,
scattering the earth with their first dramatic leaves.

                                        —*Angela Herrera*

The Wanderer

A cold grey sky, a cold grey sea
And a cold grey mist that is chilling me;
A light that burns on the harbor bar
With the dull dim glow of a distant star.
A sky without hope, a sea lacking cheer
And a beckoning light that comes not near;
The lapping of waves, the whisper of foam,
The gloom of night and a distant home.
What love can I feel for the restless sea
When all I love is leaving me!
The creak of a spar, the flap of a sail
Is far from a song since 'tis nearer a wail;
For the home and the friends that are leaving me
As I'm borne away o'er the cold grey sea.
A cold grey sky, a cold grey sea,
A distant land and a light to me
The only trace as I go my way
Of the joys and hopes of yesterday.
And I look on the sea, I turn to the sky
And they answer me life is mystery.

—Lewis H. Latimer

To Outgrow the Past

To outgrow the past but not extinguish it;
To be progressive but not raw,

Free but not mad, critical but not sterile, expectant but not
    deluded;
To be scientific but not to live on formulas that cut us off from
    life;
To hear amidst clamor the pure, deep tones of the spirit;
To seek the wisdom that liberates and a loyalty that consecrates;
To turn both prosperity and adversity into servants of
    character;
To master circumstances by the power of principle,
And to conquer death by the splendor of loving trust:
This is to attain peace;
This is to pass from drear servitude to divine adoption;
This is to invest the lowliest life with magnificence.
And to prepare it for coronation.

—William Laurence Sullivan

The Legacy of Caring

Despair is my private pain
    Born from what I have failed to say
        failed to do
        failed to overcome.
Be still my inner self
    let me rise to you
    let me reach down into your pain
    and soothe you.
I turn to you
    to renew my life

I turn to the world
    the streets of the city
        the worn tapestries of
            brokerage firms
            crack dealers
            private estates
            personal things in the bag lady's cart
        rage and pain in the faces that turn from me
            afraid of their own inner worlds.
This common world I love anew
    as the life blood of generations
        who refused to surrender their humanity
        in an inhumane world
        courses through my veins.

From within this world
    my despair is transformed to hope
    and I begin anew
    the legacy of caring.

—Thandeka

Beyond Borders

Go forth
Because we are always going forth from somewhere

Going from our homes, our childhoods
Going from our cities and countries
Going from innocence to experience to enlightenment

Going into mystery and questions
Going into the desert
Getting to the other side.

Go forth,
Leave behind the comfort and community of one place
Head into the anxiety and loneliness of another.

Carry with you the love and laughter of this place
And let it light your way
Carry with you the wisdom you learned
and the good memories
May they give you strength for your journey

And when you have been away long enough, far enough,
Done what you'd set off to do
Been there so long
That place too, starts to feel like home

Come back
Come back to the one, universal
Everywhere and every when and everyone inclusive home,
This beloved community of all creation
That you can never really leave.

—*Rick Hoyt*

REFLECTION

A Failure

"So last week I tried to hang myself on a stretch of land off I–35," said my friend, who I called my cousin.

"Jesus," I swore. "Why?"

But I already had an inkling that I knew the answer. My cousin's story wasn't very new to me anymore.

"I was tired of feeling like a failure," he said.

And there it was, the F-word.

I heard him and knew his pains like they were my own. It remains one of my greatest regrets that my scholarly father lived to see his son enter college at an early age but died before he could see him leave at a late one. In my short life I have failed at more projects than I've accomplished, and even my accomplishments don't look like much in retrospect. I work two jobs, one in a tenuous entry-level position, the other as a janitor. I have never had a romantic relationship that lasted over a year, and I drive a beat-up vehicle. Look for a picture of Success online and you will not see the face of Raziq Brown.

I have stared into The Abyss known as Failure and Loss many times. Not only has it stared back, but it has pulled me down into its murky depths just as it did my cousin, several times in fact. I have seen at least one friend claimed by The Pit, know several who are spelunking it by way of various intoxicants, and know a few more who have thrown themselves in, only to be spared by grace in its various forms.

I come from a generation of people who are often called lazy, selfish, and impractical; not unlike those from many generations before. I cringe every time I hear such things. I know there is an entire population of young people literally killing themselves to prove their inherent worth to the world and to become successful by whatever means and in whatever mode they can.

They say my generation expects too much for too little. They say we are children who refuse to grow up.

I think back on my own life, and I know they are wrong.

Would the boy I was approve of the man I am? No, the boy I was would have thrown himself off the nearest bridge just to save himself from future embarrassment. The adolescent I was would have driven the car to get him to the bridge, and the man I was the year following my father's death would have plied the boy with strong spirits so the fall wouldn't hurt so bad. But I am not the child I was, the teen I was, nor the man I was then.

I am the man I am now. It is all I can ever be. It's all any of us can be.

—Raziq George Brown

CLOSING WORDS

Life does not call us merely to do over and over again what we have already done; nor does it call us to act out, as puppets, parts already assigned to us. No. In the midst of a situation which is itself ever changing, we are free to bring into realization new relationships of understanding and good-will, and new acts of courage.

—Frank O. Holmes

To repent means to turn in a new direction— not just to admit what we have done wrong, but to resolve to be a better person.

—Jeanne Harrison Nieuwejaar

Passion and Purpose

OPENING WORDS

And heed the counsel of your own heart, for no
one is more faithful to you than it is.

— Ecclesiasticus 37:13

We are cups, constantly and quietly being filled.
The trick is, knowing how to tip ourselves over
and let the beautiful stuff out.

—Ray Bradbury

REFLECTION

Embrace

"So . . . what do you want to do with your life???"

There was a time when this question haunted me like an existential crisis. Some might call it being in my twenties, but I certainly didn't feel that such pain was just "to be expected."

I remember pouring over inspirational books. I found few answers, but I did find friends: Parker Palmer assured me that feelings of depression were not only normal but a gift that could lead me deeper and help "let my life speak." Kahlil Gibran reframed my present pain as something that was carving space for future joy. Mary Oliver proclaimed her gospel: "You do not have to be good." And Rainer Maria Rilke urged patience "with everything unresolved in (my) heart . . . to love the questions themselves." Most importantly, I learned I had good company in struggling to find my way.

Encouraged by these connections, my creative energy began to return and soon I was on the move—zigging and zagging, to be sure, but following my heart. In time, I was New York City–bound, following my dream of legal temping . . . I mean, acting. But the legal temping, along with countless early mornings, shivering in lines for theater auditions (that were already cast), *was* living the dream. I was following my passion and, in time, I began finding work.

Still, was it my *purpose*?

I remember my deep recognition watching the musical *Avenue Q* as Princeton, the protagonist puppet, opened the drama with *the* question of questions:

"What do you do with a B.A. in English?"

Princeton continues, "Everyone else has a purpose, so what's mine? . . . Gotta find out, don't wanna wait. Got to make sure that my life will be great. . . . Got to find *me*."

Fast forward—I was on the Fiftieth Anniversary European Tour of West Side Story and I was *Tony*! It was the pinnacle of my career in a role that felt meant for me. But I was struggling. We were playing Vienna, with Paris around the corner, and I was dogged by a sinus infection, struggling with the famous high notes of "Maria," and fearing the consequences. Soon they came: a ticket back home.

I was devastated. I'd overcome depression, followed my passion, and put in my time. I had practically felt the glow of my parents' pride as I imagined them watching me on stage at Le Chatelet. But it wouldn't be.

Instead . . .

I experienced love anyway.

A dear friend who'd traveled to see me holding my hand,
Cast mates' tears transforming my own,
Vienna's autumn leaves enveloping me in a golden glow,
My parents' even greater pride in my courage, facing this
    loss . . .
Words penned in a journal entry—"I am called to
    ministry."

I used to think that finding my purpose meant finding a tiny intersection point between my passion and the world's need. Then I took faith that the world needed passionate people—as Howard Thurman says, "people who have come alive."

But the greatest learning has come from feeling my fears, my losses, my dreams, and even my quest to "find me," transformed through the experience of finding and feeling *we*. Discovering my identity as one who is loved and loves passionately—*this* has been to come alive.

What do I want to do with my life? . . . Embrace it.

—*David Ruffin*

POEMS AND PRAYERS

Labyrinth

Walk the maze
within your heart: guide your steps into its questioning curves.
This labyrinth is a puzzle leading you deeper into your own
    truths.
Listen in the twists and turns.
Listen in the openness within all searching.
Listen: a wisdom within you calls to a wisdom beyond you and
    in that dialogue lies peace.

—*Leslie Takahashi Morris*

Useful Anger

A good anger swallowed
clots the blood
to slime

—Marge Piercy

But what is to be done with it,
this anger that dare not be swallowed?

Should it be diluted with denial, cooled with indifference?
Should it be sweetened with good intentions,
softened with lies?
Should it be spewed out red hot over searing tongues,
scorching the guilty and innocent alike?

What's to be done with it,
this anger that dare not be swallowed?

Don't dilute it, deny it, or cool it.
Don't sweeten it or soften it.
But, pause for a moment.

Could you hold it before your eyes
    examine it with your heart and mind?
Could you hold it
    then touch it to your belly
    that place where your soul rests?

Could you let it enter there knowing it is the part of you
  that needs to be treated kindly
  that needs to be listened to
  that needs to be honored?

For it has the power to save you,
to save us all.

—Stephen Shick

Anxiety

Fill me with anxiety, O Life!
Electrify me, make me nervous
Beyond any staid concern
For those things which challenge
Placid, flaccid ways, anachronisms of being.
Keep me tense, a-tiptoe,
Blinking at the novel,
Reaching out for those things
Just beyond my fingertips;
So that I may make patterns,
Dreams dreams, fashion worlds
Which will beat with life.
For I would be a man
And on the move.

—Arthur Graham

Uncounted Psalm

Why did I listen to Your calling, O God?
Why did I step out on faith, O Love?
Why did I lift my feet,
ignore my fear,
and run toward the unknown?
Now I am far from home.
My heart aches for my familiar land,
for people who greeted me with kisses.
I can't see the way back—it doesn't exist.
I can't see the way forward,
but I long for the place I knew.
By the time I find the way,
my children will be grown and gone.
But today You are silent.
The voice that whispered wind into my sails has stilled.
Fear rises in me like a tsunami far from shore.
Tonight, I will sleep without comfort.

—Angela Herrera

Joy

I have been wondering
what the morning glories
know. Is it envy
that compels these vines
to strangle other flowers
arising in their path?

Or perhaps self-preservation,
to climb these walls, forsaking
humbler beings, winding
greedy stems around the trellis
in their hungry pursuit of light.

Still, every morning,
basking in their spiral shadows,
I want to believe it is something more

this fevered yearning
to open purple flowers,
yield bold-throated *Glorias*
to the sun,
and in the blaze of afternoon
curl petals softly into shyness.

And every morning, I plead
with the dew-moist buds
to know their secret joy:
to open and close without holding,
to surrender all to light,
to sing
I am completely yours
over and over again.

—*Terri Pahucki*

Living Waters

We float on a sea
hidden beneath dry surfaces
covered by stones.

Isn't this why we drink and dive so deeply
go down to the sea in ships
risk drowning, again and again?

Isn't this why Moses parted the waters
to begin his journey?

Why Jesus crossed the waters
to comfort and challenge us?

We were born in water.
We float free in water.
We are washed clean by water.

Isn't this why we long to find our inward sea?
To help us wash clean the world?

—Stephen Shick

Let Me Die Laughing

We are all dying, our lives always moving toward completion.

We need to learn to live with death, and to understand that death is not the worst of all events.

We need to fear not death, but life—

empty lives,
loveless lives,
lives that do not build upon the gifts that each of us
    has been given,
lives that are like living deaths,
lives which we never take the time to savor and
    appreciate,
lives in which we never pause to breathe deeply.

What we need to fear is not death, but squandering the lives we have been miraculously given.

So let me die laughing, savoring one of life's crazy moments. Let me die holding the hand of one I love, and recalling that I tried to love and was loved in return. Let me die remembering that life has been good, and that I did what I could. But today, just remind me that I am dying so that I can live, savor, and love with all my heart.

—Mark Morrison-Reed

Self-Portrait

It doesn't interest me if there is one God
or many gods.
I want to know if you belong or feel
abandoned.
If you can know despair or can see it in others.
I want to know
if you are prepared to live in the world

with its harsh need
to change you. If you can look back
with firm eyes
saying this is where I stand. I want to know
if you know
how to melt into that fierce heat of living
falling toward
the center of your longing. I want to know
if you are willing
to live, day by day, with the consequence of love
and the bitter
unwanted passion of your sure defeat.

I have been told, in *that* fierce embrace, even
the gods speak of God.

—David Whyte

REFLECTION

The Road We Travel Together

I've always had a tough time falling asleep. As a child, I was skeptical about the whole idea of sleep. I thought, "Who needs it anyway? Can't we just be awake all the time? Isn't that what life is all about?" So it is not surprising that, when my now mother-in-law asked me a few years ago whether I was a morning person or a night person, I responded simply and with great enthusiasm, "I'm a people person!" I love being with people in religious and secular contexts, participating in fun, social justice, and community service activities; there is always something meaningful to be done. Sleep, on the other hand, has always seemed like such a waste of time—a third of our lives right down the drain in a state of lethargic inaction. However, as I have grown into a young man, I realize that something magical happens in the time just before and during sleep. We are offered a rare opportunity to sort through the noisiness and distractions of our lives to arrive at a place where we can hear the silent prayers of our hearts and of the world. And I believe it's in this silence before sleep that we are able to touch the most authentic piece of our identities and of our dreams for the future.

As young adults, we live in a precarious time when our identities and dreams for the future are clouded by the half-fulfilled/half-crushed dreams of past generations. We are bombarded by warring expectations about how we should live our lives and what we should do to benefit the social order. However, among all of my experiences with friends from school and work, from church and my neighborhood, I see a pattern in these young dreams and deep prayers.

Our dream is not just to take Robert Frost's road less traveled but to proclaim that this is the road we must travel together. We dream and pray for a new way of being in relationship with one another, both in our churches and in all the communities we engage with locally, nationally, and internationally. As young people, we are reimagining the kind of world we seek to create together in the twenty-first century. For we are the dreamers of dreams that have been passed down for millennia, dreams that affirm an eternal belief in a world that is yet to be created but is surely emerging around us every day. We have faith in a world that celebrates the diversity and sacredness of life and works toward the liberation and happiness of all. Unitarian Universalist young adults are engaging in the important conversations about how our identities as individuals and as a faith community must ignite in us an urge to dream a little bigger, pray a little louder, and cherish those few moments before sleep when we can touch the divinity within our hearts and in the world.

—*Nic Cable*

CLOSING WORDS

There is a life-force within your soul, seek
    that life.
There is a gem in the mountain of your body,
    seek that mine.
O traveler, if you are in search of That
Don't look outside, look inside yourself and
    seek That.

—Rumi

Take it, then, as a general principle to be
observed as one of the directing impulses of
life that you must have some great purpose
of existence . . . to make your talents and your
knowledge most beneficial to your country
and most useful to mankind.

—John Quincy Adams

Community

OPENING WORDS

We are different so that we can know our need of one another, for no one is ultimately self-sufficient. The completely self-sufficient person would be subhuman.

—Desmond Tutu

What should young people do with their lives today? Many things, obviously. But the most daring thing is to create stable communities in which the terrible disease of loneliness can be cured.

—Kurt Vonnegut

REFLECTION

Show Up Hungry

I got off work at 7 PM and did the thing where you chase the bus a little bit but then realize you won't make it and walk sheepishly back to the bus stop. I'm already an hour late to Sunday night singing at the Lucy Stone Cooperative, a UU affordable housing co-op in Boston. I'm still ambivalent—I could go home to Netflix and grilled cheese. I could choose predictability and warm carbs. Or I could get on the bus to this community where I was first a member of the planning team and now a board member, this place where, despite my leadership role, I still find myself questioning whether and how I belong.

I give myself a little pep talk, reminding myself that I'm allowed to show up late and hungry and in need of a song. Reminding myself that being in community means offering care and being cared for, bringing my shiny self and my not-so-shiny self.

When I arrive, there's a teapot of hot water and a plate of fat dates on the table. A friend presses a bowl into my hands and there's broccoli soup. We sing "Amazing Grace": "The wonders of accepting love have made me whole and real."

Community is covenant. It's the promise of a bowl of soup and a song at the end of the day. It's love in the form of a house on Moreland Street that has said that it doesn't matter that I don't live there, that I too am welcome on Sunday nights. Laid bare, it is the succor and accountability of doing that thing together that we cannot do alone.

I've not always been my best self in the communities I've loved. I've shirked dish duty at Lucy Stone and missed weddings in my home town. I've dropped out when I was needed and showed up full of pettiness and exhaustion. The wonder of accepting love is only made evident when we're allowed to shed the shiny and let the sourness show. Our communities of spirit are only real because we show up late expecting to be fed. Because we both give and get. Because we bring our tart and our sweet, our gifts and our struggles. We need lemon in the lentils, rice vinegar in the sushi, a squeeze of lime in the chelada, and some acid in our communities. Without it, our communities are superficial. With no acid, we are one-note, monotone. Our vulnerabilities, our bits of brokenness, bring life to our relationships.

We are part of community when we show up shiny and not-so-shiny. When we ladle soup into each other's bowls and eat it eagerly. When we bring our sour and our sweet. When we shed the shiny and show up hungry.

—*Elizabeth Nguyen*

POEMS AND PRAYERS

Flawless

For far too many years
I have wanted to be flawless,
   Perfecting my pursuits,
   I bargained all for love.

For all these many years
I've made masks of my own doing,
   Pursuing my perfection,
   I found I was pursued.

And then
one day
I fell
   sprawled
   flattened
   lost

on the fertile ground of self.

Naked in dirt
no mask
no bargains

I raised my soiled face
   and there
   you were.

I struggled to stand.

Dirt from my body
clouded your eyes.
Your hand reached
for me.
Blinded,
your
hand
reached
me.

There is, in all of us, a place of pure perfection.
We discover its geography together.

—*Margaret Wheatley*

In Gatherings

In gatherings we are stirred
like the leaves of the fall season
rustling around sacred trees,
tossed hither and yon
until we come to rest together,
quietly, softly . . .

We come to gather strength from each other.
We come to give strength to each other.
We come to ask for strength from the Spirit of All That Is
    and Is Not.

When our hearts sing or when they frown
it is the way of compassion telling us to give.
It is the way of peace telling us
to share our gifts,
for we are happiest
and most powerful
when Love is made apparent
in and through us.

Spirit of the circle that is Love,
as we twirl in this dance that is life
we give thanks for reminding us each day
of our task of ministering to each "other"
with a searching glance,
a safe touch,
a generous smile,
a thoughtful word . . .

Thank you for reminding us
that we are always building our beloved *comunidad*.

Thank you for reminding us
that through our covenant with you

we covenant with each "other"
and are made whole.

In gratitude, we celebrate
with open hearts and minds.
We discover who we are,
separate from each other
and within one another.

In this circle that holds all life
may we ever work toward
widening its boundaries
until there are none.

Amen. Paz. Blessed Be.

        —Marta I. Valentín

Meditation on Opposites

Spirit of the universe,
Life force that flows through all beings,
Power beyond our knowing,

We ask you to help us see beyond our dependence on opposites—
To transcend our desire to know who is like us, and who is not.

Open us to the knowledge that in this room
there are complexities and diversities of identities
beyond black and white,

old and young,
woman and man,
poor and rich,
uneducated and educated,
disabled and able-bodied,
gay and straight,
ill and healthy,
wrong and right,
broken and whole.

In this room there are people who embody juxtaposition,
who can tell stories written on their bodies about *both* and
    neither,
who carry intimate pieces of the truth that there is
no such thing
as opposites.

Spirit of many names and of no name at all,
Help us find release from our belief that all things must be
    either/or,
this belief that walls us off from one another,
ensnaring us in a battle of same versus different.

Help us to open our minds,
to deeply listen,
and to truly know one another,
finally glimpsing the kaleidoscopic beauty of the divine.

—*Alex Kapitan*

Part as Parcel

I am part of you, O Truth Unfolding.
I am part of you.
I am part of a cosmos.
I cannot see
either its edge or its end.
How amazing!
I am part of a galaxy of a million, billion stars.
They say it's a pinwheel.
How wonderful!
I am part of a system of planets that swing
around a small parent star. How strong the hands
of invisible gravity must be
to hold it all together, just so!
I am part of a planet, green and blue,
along with mountains and seas,
sponges and spores,
lichen and lava,
robins and rain,
periwinkles and perch,
centipedes and cities.
How great the variety!
How astonishing the mutual dependence of it all!
I am part of a species
that belongs to a grouping of animals
called mammalia
and so is every other human being, equally so.

I am part of a political unit called a nation.
There are many nations,
each of them dear in many ways
to its local citizens.
I am part of a family with ethnicity, practice,
and love in the form of food,
rooted in the mountains of Emilia.
Others know other roots, other practices.
I am part of a circle of friends rooted,
not in ethnicity or food,
but in simple redemptive love.
I am part of a climate region,
part of a state,
part of a city,
part of a neighborhood,
part of a congregation,
and part of a staff.
And with you I am part and parcel of this moment,
this simple silence which lasts but a few breaths,
and then is gone forever.
But like cosmos, galaxy, planet, species, nation, climate, city,
    neighborhood, family, and
circles of friendship, it
is precious,
a present for which I give thanks.

—*Mark Belletini*

The Web of Life

There is a living web that runs through us
To all the universe,
Linking us each with each and through all life
On to the distant stars.
Each knows a little corner of the world, and lives
As if this were the all.
We no more see the farther reaches of the threads
Than we see of the future, yet they're there.
Touch but one thread, no matter which;
The thoughtful eye may trace to distant lands
Its firm continuing strand, yet lose its filaments as they
    reach out,
But find at last it coming back to the place from which it led.
We move as in a fog, aware of self
But only dimly conscious of the rest
As they are close to us in sight or feeling.
New objects loom up for a time, fade in and out;
Then, sometimes, as we look on unawares, the fog lifts
And there's the web in shimmering beauty,
Reaching past all horizons. We catch our breath;
Stretch out our eager hands, and then
In comes the fog again, and we go on,
Feeling a little foolish, doubting what we had seen.
The hands were right. The web is real.
Our folly is that we so soon forget.

—*Robert T. Weston*

We never know who we are

We never know who we are
(this is strange, isn't it?)

or what vows we made
or who we knew

or what we hoped for
or where we were

when the world's dreams
were seeded.

Until the day just one of us

sighs a gentle longing
and we all feel the change

one of us calls a name
and we all know to be there

one of us tells a dream
and we all breathe life into it

one of us asks "why?"
and we all know the answer.

It is very strange.

We never know who we are.

—*Margaret Wheatley*

Meditation on Broken Hearts

Let us enter into a time of meditation, contemplation, and
      prayer.
Feel the earth beneath your feet as it supports you.
Feel the love of this community as it surrounds and enfolds
      you.
Feel your breath as it flows in
   and out of your body.
Listen to your heartbeat.
Listen to your heart . . .

And how is it with your heart?
Does your heart feel whole, shielded by intellect, cocooned
      by reason,
   closed to feeling?
Or is it broken, fragile to the touch, brimming with the pain
      of loss?

Or has your heart been broken and healed so many times
   that it now lies open to the world,
   knowing that true growth comes not without pain,
   that tears may wear down barriers,
   that we may carry the hearts of others
   even when our own is too heavy for us to bear.

None of us has an unblemished heart, not one.
For such perfection can be found only in death,
   and we who are alive still have much to heal.

So let us give thanks for the broken places in our hearts,
    and in our lives.
For it is only through such brokenness that we may truly touch
    one another
    and only through touching one another that the world may
    be healed.

Let us give then thanks for the brokenness that we share.

—Tom Rhodes

We Meet on Holy Ground

We meet on holy ground,
Brought into being as life encounters life,
As personal histories merge into the communal story,
As we take on the pride and pain of our companions,
As separate selves become community.

How desperate is our need for one another:
Our silent beckoning to our neighbors,
Our invitations to share life and death together,
Our welcome into the lives of those we meet,
And their welcome into our own.

May our souls capture this treasured time.
May our spirits celebrate our meeting
In this time and in this space,
For we meet on holy ground.

—Richard S. Gilbert

REFLECTION

The Grout

The Unitarian Universalist congregation where I served as an intern made a mosaic Tree of Life the summer before I arrived. Congregants of all ages came together to craft the tree's leaves, using bits and pieces of broken ceramics, jewelry, glass, and stone. There are many precious personal items in the tree, including fragments of the Berlin Wall, a father's watch face, pieces of great grandmother's china, and a key to the front door of a loved home. Like the members of the community that brought them together, each part is imbued with memories and meaning; each fragment holds a piece of truth.

Unitarian Universalists are mosaic makers. We are a people who bring together the broken pieces of our histories and the shining pieces of our seeking and, piece by piece, create a mosaic religion. Our Tree of Life is found in the stories of our living tradition. The bead from a transformational moment of worship at a youth conference. The bit of paper stamped with the blazing emblem of the Unitarian Service Committee that saved lives during World War II. The button or patch on a backpack that proudly proclaims the first justice issue that lit our souls on fire. But our mosaic making tells another story too, one that is often more difficult to see. One that is essential to the purpose of religious community. One that lies not in the beautiful and broken bits and pieces but in the grout.

Grout. The chalky, gritty stuff that is squeezed between the cracks of tiles. In a mosaic, the grout holds the image together, unifying disparate pieces into a whole. The grout of a community takes years to lay and settle. Grout happens in board meetings and committee meetings and endless emails and slow-moving institutions. It is in weekly potlucks shared by neighbors, a ride to church, and coffee in the social hall after worship. While the folks who show up for church only on Christmas and Easter will hopefully enjoy the beauty of the mosaic they find, they may never know the power of the grout that holds us through all the seasons of life.

We help to make the grout when we learn each other's names and when we reach out across generational divides. We help to make the grout when we show up on Sunday morning without having checked first to see if we're interested in the sermon topic. When a newborn arrives to be blessed by the community, it is the grout that enables us to welcome them. And it is in the grout that we rest when we gather to grieve and memorialize a beloved one who has died.

Hold us, O Grout.

Gather us in, through time and space, and make all our broken pieces whole in community. In our multiplicity, make us one. From each of our jagged edges, give us the shape of a communal beauty.

—Marcus Liefert

CLOSING WORDS

The universe sings no less
because time and space
wear us thin.

The music calls us
to recognize our limitations,
to recognize that
the song is best
sung with others.

—*Manish K. Mishra-Marzetti*

Take courage, friends.
    The way is often hard,
    the path is never clear,
    and the stakes are very high.
Take courage, for deep down, there is another truth:
    You are not alone.

—*Wayne B. Arnason*

Roots

OPENING WORDS

There's an old saying about those who forget
history. I don't remember it, but it's good.

—Stephen Colbert

We are our past and our tradition, as it meets
the future.

—Carl Scovel

REFLECTION

What We Choose

A few years ago, my little sister moved in with me from our native Los Angeles to the coast of Maine. The move brought a lot of firsts for her: snow, the Atlantic Ocean, and seeing me as an older brother instead of an older sister.

Neither of us was sure what to do that first night she lived with me because what are you supposed to do when, at twenty-two, you suddenly have your very own teenager?

We ended up at one of those DVD kiosks; when it asked for my ZIP Code I punched the number 9 before correcting myself and typing the 0 that starts off the ZIP Code for Bar Harbor.

"Still?" my sister asked.

I'd started the ZIP Code for back home. It had been ten years since I moved away. My sister's arrival brought part of my past into my very different present. And this suddenly forced everything out of the hiding places I'd been keeping them in. I had put home into a box and stuffed it into the farthest depths of my closet. I got lost without it for a while, but then I found communities that seemed to make sense in a way my family never did.

I used to scoff at the idea of chosen family because it seemed like a feel-good characterization to use when your family of origin didn't work for you. I never really embraced it for myself until I started thinking about *ancestry* rather than parentage.

Like so many people my age in the United States, my identities are all mixed up and only partially visible. The more mixed up our identities get, the more important our choices become. Ancestry is no longer just a question of fate or genetics but of whose shoulders we stand on. My genetic families of origin aren't necessarily recognizable when you look at me. But my chosen family—those queers and religious liberals of the past, present, and future—come shining through. I embody that history when I walk out the door because they made it *possible* for me to walk out the door as an openly transgender seminarian. They are my history more completely than anything I was born into. I used to think that meant family of choice was no place to call home, but it's not that simple.

Every time we move toward liberation we can do so because of those who came before us. Those who come after us will move more easily because of what we have accomplished. This is not something limited to queer people whose families are giving them a hard time. We all choose. And sometimes that dividing line between choice and birth disappears.

My sister never embraced the East Coast the way I did. She moved back "home," but we talk now. She'll text me, "hey bro." We've chosen each other. Just as we've found different ancestors to lean on and have established our own networks of support. We've chosen different todays, are making different tomorrows, and have different pasts. Yet we also share a common history—and now we are a part of each other's todays and tomorrows as well.

—*Andrew Coate*

POEMS AND PRAYERS

Returning

I Years had been from Home
And now before the Door
I dared not enter, lest a Face
I never saw before

Stare stolid into mine
And ask my Business there –
"My Business but a Life I left
Was such remaining there?"

I leaned upon the Awe –
I lingered with Before –
The Second like an Ocean rolled
And broke against my ear –

I laughed a crumbling Laugh –
That I could fear a Door
Who Consternation compassed
And never winced before.

I fitted to the Latch
My Hand, with trembling care
Lest back the awful Door should spring
And leave me in the Floor –

Then moved my Fingers off
As cautiously as Glass
And held my ears, and like a Thief
Fled gasping from the House –

—Emily Dickinson

The Blue Chinese Bowl

Mother owned a blue and white Chinese bowl
    so large it might have held mountains
    of sharp-crowned pineapples, sunrise peaches,
        ripe pears.
It might have held bunches of roses, pink, ivory,
    flowing over its sides, dropping petals on the
        table.
Perhaps it was full enough with stories of the Colonel's wife,
    her estate watched by Grandpa, her gardens
        fragrant.
White porcelain elegantly brushed with blue chrysanthemums,
    perhaps this bowl needed nothing.

When mother got divorced she ran quickly from our small house,
    leaving her china but she took the bowl,
    and as I grew she said, "Someday it will be yours."
In ugly houses warped with rage
    it opened serenely.
When I was grown and she moved again, she sold it.
    "Why?" I screamed. "You promised."

But she couldn't say.
The bowl has stuck in memory,
    hard with anger.

Mother's gone, the question discarded
    with many others.
Now I give away anger, blue chrysanthemums,
    falling petals.

—Leone Scanlon

We Are

For each child that's born, a morning star rises and sings to the
    universe who we are.
We are our grandmothers' prayers and
we are our grandfathers' dreamings,
we are the breath of our ancestors,
we are the spirit of God.
We are mothers of courage and fathers of time,
we are daughters of dust and the sons of great visions,
we're sisters of mercy and brothers of love,
we are lovers of life and the builders of nations,
we're seekers of truth and keepers of faith,
we are makers of peace and the wisdom of ages.

—Ysaye M. Barnwell

Spiritual History

Let my body remember.
Let my hands and feet remember.
Let my breath remember
those who have come before me,
those who have come before us.
Didn't Muhammad wait quietly in his cave?
And didn't Jesus sigh silently by the blue lake?
And Guan Yin, didn't she sit in silence
thinking about what to do before doing it?
And what was Siddhartha the Buddha doing
anyway under that tree if not just sitting quietly?
And Susan B. Anthony, didn't she push back
from her desk, and take a breath now and then?
And Florence Nightingale, didn't she
put down her nurse's hat
and think silently about what to write
in her essay on mysticism before she actually wrote it?
And Sophia Fahs, didn't she stop telling
stories sometimes and just sit there?
And didn't Black Elk just notice the sunlight
glancing off his chair sometimes?
And Starhawk, does she only talk and write, or
does she too keep silence?
Let us remember them all with our bodies.
Let us remember them with the silence
they too knew.

—Mark Belletini

It Is That Time and That Place

Now is the time to call on the memories of the ancestors who thought they could not walk another step toward freedom—and yet they did.

It is that time and place to call on the memories of the ancestors who, when the darkness of their lives threatened to take away the hope and light, reached a little deeper and prayed yet another prayer.

It is that time and place to remember those who came through the long night to witness another sunrise.

It is that time and place to remember the oceans of tears shed to deliver us to this time, to remember the bent knees and bowed backs, to remember the fervent voices asking, begging and beseeching for loved ones sold off.

Time to remember their laughter and joy, though they had far less, and little reason for optimism, yet they stayed on the path toward a better day.

Time to hold to the steadfast hands and hearts and prayers of the ancestors that have brought us this far.

Time to make them proud and show them, and ourselves, what we are made of.

Time to show them that their prayers and sacrifices and lives were not in vain and did not go unnoticed, nor have they been forgotten.

Did you not know that this day would come?
Did you not know that we would have to change places?
Did you not know that just as our ancestors were delivered that you would also be delivered?

Have you not seen the greatness and power of the Creative Energy in the Universe called God that moves and has its being through human agency?

Have you not seen God in your neighbors' faces? In the homeless? In the battered woman? The trafficked child? The undocumented worker? The dispossessed? It is that time and that place to know that it is our turn, that we must leave a legacy for our children. And all the children.

It is that time and that place.
We are the ones we've been waiting for!
For that, let us be eternally grateful.
Amen and Blessed Be.

—Qiyamah Rahman

Love Abundant

I lift my eyes up to the hills
from where will my help come?
My help comes from Love abundant.
my help comes from the hills
my help—my help, it comes from
ancient Mothers whose hearts beat in mine.
It comes from the trees that sway and the breeze that sways
    them . . .
my help comes from all that was and is and will ever be . . .
I lift my eyes . . . hushed by the soothing touch of waves
caressing wounded shores
wounded souls
I lift my eyes . . . to the horizon bathed by
the hum of mothers and mothers' mothers
cradling—gently rocking
I lift my voice—call of the sea trees sister moon mother earth
my soul weeping—a symphony of life overflowing
I give myself
I too hum through every pore
with every breath
I give myself—
an extension
of all that is, was, and ever will be.

—*Alicia R. Forde*

I call upon you

I call upon you, *<ancestor>*,
from the Cloud of Witnesses to accompany me today.

You teach me *<value(s)>*,
and today I am called to *<action/mission>*.

Walk with me.
Inspire me.

Hold me accountable so I may bring honor to you,
amplify love and compassion to those around me,
and make the way easier for those yet to come.

I ask this because you are mine
and I am yours.

You live in me
and I live in you.

Amen.

—Tandi Rogers

They Are with Us Still

In the struggles we choose for ourselves,
in the ways we move forward in our lives
and bring our world forward with us,

It is right to remember the names of those
who gave us strength in this choice of living.
It is right to name the power of hard lives well-lived.

We share a history with those lives.
We belong to the same motion.

They too were strengthened by what had gone before.
They too were drawn on by the vision of what might come
    to be.

Those who lived before us,
who struggled for justice and suffered injustice before us,
have not melted into the dust,
and have not disappeared.

They are with us still.
The lives they lived hold us steady.

Their words remind us and call us back to ourselves.
Their courage and love evoke our own.

We, the living, carry them with us:
we are their voices, their hands and their hearts.

We take them with us,
and with them choose the deeper path of living.

—Kathleen McTigue

REFLECTION

We Are Community

The history and legacy of Unitarian Universalism are shaped as much by Emerson, Fahs, and Channing as it is by the ancestors in our congregations. We come to it through different avenues: the Internet, an invitation, reading the Transcendentalists, or as babies or little kids.

I came as a fourth grader to my congregation, the Tennessee Valley Unitarian Universalist Church in Knoxville, Tennessee (TVUUC). This community helped bring me into social justice struggles in the world around me and inside the UUA. They brought me as a child to the place where I now work, the Highlander Center. My church opened so many doors because they held young people in high esteem and encouraged our leadership in the church and community. I will never forget going to our district's Journey Toward Wholeness Transformation Team meeting (the UUA's anti-racism program) and realizing that I was the youngest person there by nearly fifteen years.

My religious education teachers, friends' parents, and spirit aunts and uncles were and still are community leaders in everything from nuclear disarmament to anti-racism/anti-oppression issues. They protested U.S. military involvement in Central America and stood behind the parent of a classmate as she transitioned from male to female in the early nineties. They have been my inspiration as I work to support others who are called by their faith to change hearts, minds, and communities.

My church changed forever on July 27, 2008, when an armed man came into the sanctuary and killed two UU leaders, one a member of TVUUC and the other a member of Westside Church. This rocked our church to its core. When I first heard about it, I didn't know who had been killed—my mom, my friends and their parents, or others who had nurtured me my entire life. I realized something that day that has stayed with me ever since: No matter what issues I have with other Unitarian Universalists regarding our visions of God/Spirit, justice, race, and age—at the root of everything is community, love, and faith. That day, something larger than our individual beliefs rose up in my mind. I thought of the principles, values, and family that are the connective tissue of our faith community and that held us weeks after the shooting, six months later on our sixtieth anniversary, and still today.

I am part of the connective tissue that holds the legacy and future of our faith. I am Church Across the Street, AYS, YRUU, youth cons, Journey Toward Wholeness, GROUNDWORK, C*UUYAN, the Mountain, and GA Youth and Young Adult Caucus.

We are the children of freedom fighters, visionaries, and radical liberal theologians.

We are the phoenix rising out of the ashes of the McCarthy era and the civil rights, women's, and queer liberation movements.

We are the survivors and beneficiaries of youth-led and youth-focused beliefs and programming that encouraged us to be change makers, boundary pushers, and institutionalists at the same time.

We are and will be the ministers, religious educators, congregational presidents, organizers, and social change leaders our faith has led us to be.

We wear our faith as tattoos on our bodies and in our hearts as testaments to the blood, tears, dreams, and inspirations of our community ancestors and elders.

—*Elandria Williams*

CLOSING WORDS

Don't forget who you are and where you come from.

—F. Scott Fitzgerald

As our lives span the years, so do they intercept and interlock with one another that the generations seem not to be separate, but one. In their deeds and actions, their interests and motivations, the women of the past are as much a part of us today as they were in the beginning.

—Laura Hersey

Family, Friends, and Loves

OPENING WORDS

This is my commandment, that you love one another as I have loved you. No one has greater love than this, to lay down one's life for one's friends.

—*John 15:12–13*

Love is knotted and gnarled, like an old tree fighting with the wind, like branches too brittle for their own good, like roots that relentlessly inform how deeply we can trust and how freely we can forgive.

—*Jan Carlsson-Bull*

REFLECTION

No One Tells You

There was a period in my life when, within three months, all my major relationships changed. The most joyous of these was getting married; Sarah and I had dated for three and a half years, and I proposed to her at our holiday party. People tend to shine the spotlight on proposals, which makes them seem as if they happen all at once, but really they take much longer. I decided a year prior that I wanted to be married to Sarah, and spent a year in discernment. For all the relationship advice out there, it's impossible to find anything helpful on the most basic decision of all—whether to commit to spend the rest of your life with someone.

We married in the First Unitarian Universalist Church of Columbus, where we were both active members, surrounded by friends and family who loved us so dearly. It served as a fitting goodbye because we moved across the country two weeks later.

They say that moving is one of the most stressful transitions of life, but that misses the point. The stressful part isn't the saying goodbye or the move itself. It is the ripping of your life away from its roots, and it plays out over months and years. Setting new life patterns, finding new friends—these things take time and require soul work. You have to go out and make them happen. No one tells you that.

Two months after we moved, my parents, who had been married for thirty-one years, called us up on a Sunday afternoon and said, in a matter-of-fact sort of way, that they were getting divorced. I grieved, as I hadn't grieved for anything or anyone before, over the loss of our nuclear family. Here again, the 1.67 gazillion metric tons of advice and self-help books were totally useless for an adult child of divorcing parents. Surely I can't be the only one?

Like moving, my parents' divorce started with a dramatic shift, but the real change and struggle occurred over time. It forced me to question the assumptions upon which I had based my life. Should I make sacrifices for my career? Or should my partner's needs sometimes take priority? How can I raise a family and still maintain my own well-being, or my marriage? Is there such a thing as security? How do we keep in touch with that which is deepest and most profound in us?

When I imagined what all these transitions would mean, I focused on my relationships with other people. Yet the most profound changes have been the internal ones that touched the core of my being and belief. Re-examining the principles that guide my life has given me a new take on my constantly evolving understanding of the person I want to become and the relationships I want to have. It has been a labor of love, if sometimes a lonely one. No one said it would be easy. And this time, they were right.

—Carey McDonald

POEMS AND PRAYERS

Gentleness in Living

Be gentle with another—

It is a cry from the lives of people battered
By thoughtless words and brutal deeds;
It comes from the lips of those who speak them,
And the lives of those who do them.

Who of us can look inside another and know what is there
Of hope and hurt, or promise and pain?
Who can know from what far places each has come
Or to what far places each may hope to go?

Our lives are like fragile eggs.
They crack and the substance escapes.
Handle with care!
Handle with exceedingly tender care
For there are human beings within,
Human beings as vulnerable as we are,
Who feel as we feel,
Who hurt as we hurt.

Life is too transient to be cruel with one another;
It is too short for thoughtlessness,
Too brief for hurting.

Life is long enough for caring,
It is lasting enough for sharing,
Precious enough for love.

Be gentle with one another.

—*Richard S. Gilbert*

New People Came This Time

New People came this time, and we shared
our stories, the familiar truths, about
shock and healing and being glad that at last
our children can say who they are,
and we know them now, love them more.

Funny stories and good news ripple around,
and smiles about lesbigay ways, and jokes,
against ourselves, taking the masks off
to show the same donkey faces underneath.
A communion of laughter.

And several dawns once more lit up among us,
the sharpness of beginning sight,
a slower sunrise over the years,
other eye-openings—painful or proud—all good.
A communion of wisdom.

But this time—

we nearly all wept:
wept with the blinding new hurts,
winced with what we thought
had been healed—old wounds, waiting.
We put the tissue box in the middle
and passed it round.
A communion of tears.

—*Geoffrey Herbert*

Those Winter Sundays

Sundays too my father got up early
and put his clothes on in the blueblack cold,
then with cracked hands that ached
from labor in the weekday weather made
banked fires blaze. No one ever thanked him.

I'd wake and hear the cold splintering, breaking.
When the rooms were warm, he'd call,
and slowly I would rise and dress,
fearing the chronic angers of that house,

Speaking indifferently to him,
who had driven out the cold
and polished my good shoes as well.
What did I know, what did I know
of love's austere and lonely offices?

—*Robert Hayden*

The Bath

This is what one hundred years look like:
A rounded wrinkled back,
sparkling wet and soapy above the shower bench,
and my hand,
having gently formed in your seventieth year,
and emerged with lifelines bent toward blessing,
scrubbing circles across your soft, white skin.

I drag the cloth beneath your arms,
silently blessing each bend and crease
of breasts and belly, whose curves were determined
in the womb
of my great great
grandmother.

When you are dry and warm,
one hundred mantras of gratitude
sweep over my heart
that I am the one standing in the frosted light,
rubbing wisps of fragrant talcum into each sweet fold.

Tomorrow I return to Boston,
and you'll keep on in your chair
by the picture window
looking down at Seattle.
You are too old to tell your stories now
and have all but ceased speaking,

your thank you honeys
like gems at a silent retreat.

But the stories have become me,
the lifelines that led to my lifelines,
and your name was mine
long before I was dreamed
and was born.

For now there's no reason
to talk.
I adorn you with perfume and color.
Powder, lipstick, rouge.
We get out the pearls.
Looking down at your toenails,
with a fresh coat of glittery red,
you erupt in laughter.

Will you have to take it off?

All day I kiss you
as often as I can
without making you suspicious
that I'm saying goodbye,
knowing that when you're gone,
I will rise a generation.
And as storylines are lifelines,
I too shall pass them on.

—*Angela Herrera*

Friendship

Oh, the comfort—the inexpressible comfort of feeling *safe* with a person—having neither to weigh thoughts nor measure words, but pouring them all right out, just as they are, chaff and grain together; certain that a faithful hand will take and sift them, keep what is worth keeping, and then with the breath of kindness blow the rest away.

—Dinah Maria Mulock Craik

Give All to Love

Give all to love;
Obey thy heart;
Friends, kindred, days,
Estate, good-fame,
Plans, credit and the Muse,—
Nothing refuse.

'T is a brave master;
Let it have scope:
Follow it utterly,
Hope beyond hope.
It was never for the mean;
It requireth courage stout.
Souls above doubt,
Valor unbending,
It will reward,—

They shall return
More than they were,
And ever ascending.

—*Ralph Waldo Emerson*

Faults

They came to tell your faults to me,
They named them over one by one;
I laughed aloud when they were done,
I knew them all so well before,—
Oh, they were blind, too blind to see
Your faults had made me love you more.

—*Sara Teasdale*

Where We Belong, A Duet

In every town and village,
In every city square,
In crowded places
I searched the faces
Hoping to find
Someone to care.

I read mysterious meanings
In the distant stars,
Then I went to schoolrooms

And poolrooms
And half-lighted cocktail bars.
Braving dangers,
Going with strangers,
I don't even remember their names.
I was quick and breezy
And always easy
Playing romantic games.

I wined and dined a thousand exotic Joans and Janes
In dusty dance halls, at debutante balls,
On lonely country lanes.
I fell in love forever,
Twice every year or so.
I wooed them sweetly, was theirs completely,
But they always let me go.
Saying bye now, no need to try now,
You don't have the proper charms.
Too sentimental and much too gentle
I don't tremble in your arms.

Then you rose into my life
Like a promised sunrise.
Brightening my days with the light in your eyes.
I've never been so strong,
Now I'm where I belong.

—Maya Angelou

REFLECTION

Saying Yes

By the time I was in my late twenties, I was convinced that I would never find love. I had had a few boyfriends, but over and over again, I was exiled to the dreaded Friend Zone. I always suspected that it was because I was "too much": too smart, too feminist, too radical, too fat, too independent, too big of a personality. After a while, I reached the conclusion that I would just have to get used to the idea of being "too much" all by myself.

But then I met Karen: nearly six feet tall, older, black, brilliant, stylishly butch, fiercely outspoken and opinionated, and funny as hell. (And, it turns out, also a UU minister.) We became quick friends, and the "too-much-ness" in each of us somehow wasn't threatening or diminishing to either of us but instead created something vibrant and life-giving.

Karen was the one who pursued me (much to my surprise). Although I had only dated cisgender men before, it wasn't Karen's sex that gave me pause—I had been raised in a UU family and congregation that had taught me that love is love, whatever body or gender it comes in. It was our other differences: the fact that she had a daughter, that she was already deep in the thick of ministry and I was just getting started, that she was older than the partner I had imagined for myself, that interracial relationships are always complex. Could I say yes to this, knowing that if one of my friends had come to me for advice about a similar situation, I might have told them to run screaming in the other direction?

But my gut and my heart told me that there was something important and real and beautiful between us. I realized that to say yes to this relationship wouldn't be an act of reason but an act of faith—and that *my* faith, rooted deep in our UU tradition, was telling me to not let convention prevent me from connection, to take risks that nurture relationship over isolation, to remember that we are all worthy of love, and that it is ours to claim if we are but brave enough to answer its call.

Five years later, that faith full choice is one of the best I have ever made. I never expected, at this point in my life (thirty-two years old now), to be the parent of a fabulous teenager, the partner of a middle-aged goofball, or a member of this chaotic, rowdy, tightly knit, compassionate network of chosen and original family that, somehow, affirms and celebrates that very "too much-ness" that I thought might leave me forever alone. Our relationship is rooted in deep values of trust, respect, mutuality, celebration, challenge, and joy, and it is life-giving. I am profoundly grateful for the faith that formed me, bringing that "yes" to my lips in spite of all that would have discouraged that choice.

At the end of my life, as one of my favorite hymns says, "If they ask what I did best, tell them I said 'yes' to love."

—*Ashley Horan*

CLOSING WORDS

The emotion of love, in spite of the romantics, is not self-sustaining; it endures only when the lovers love many things together, and not merely each other.

—Walter Lippmann

Love changes, and in change is true.

—Wendell Berry

Identity

OPENING WORDS

Wisdom, fundamentally, is knowing who you are, where you are, and what you're trying to do or be.

—*Gordon B. McKeeman*

Each of us is meant to have a character all our own, to be what no other can exactly be, and do what no other can exactly do.

—*William Ellery Channing*

REFLECTION

I Realized

I realized I was a woman, or more precisely at the time, a girl, the day in first grade I noticed boys were looking up my dress when I was on the monkey bars. I started wearing shorts under my dresses. I now prefer pants.

I realized I liked other women when I was nineteen and noticed I was heartbroken when my friend, who burned a hole in my jacket with her clove cigarette the year before, was no longer in school. I started kissing a lot of people; I now have an amazing girlfriend.

I realized I was white when I was twenty-two and noticed the invisible backpack of privilege I carried around. I started reading a lot about race. I'm still reading now, and am adjusting my actions and interactions accordingly.

This, of course, is not an exhaustive list of my identities. I could add cisgender and middle class; I could add daughter and lover. When I look at my many identities, I am struck by how old I was when I truly realized the privilege of being white, and how young I was when I understood the oppression of being a woman. Although the discrimination I faced because of my gender hit me in the face pretty early, privilege is a part of my identity and a reality of my culture I could not have figured out on my own.

I am grateful to Unitarian Universalism for helping me develop and analyze my identities. This faith has helped me deal with the oppression I face, and realize the privilege I have. I am grateful that my religion has fostered and spurred my development and pushed me to develop aspects of myself as I could not have done alone. By growing older amid the support of this community, I have realized many aspects of my identity. I am still growing into them. I'd like to think that I'm a more out queer woman last year than I was five years ago, a more racially aware white person this year than I was last year, and that I will be a stronger woman tomorrow than I am today.

The sad yet relieving truth about all of these identities is this: I'm not good at being any *one* of them. And I probably never will be. Yet it is helpful for me to think about these different aspects of myself, so I intentionally develop my different parts and maintain balance.

I am still growing into my many identities, and for that, I am grateful. I know I will never perfectly be any one of them, and so I'll keep growing and getting better at being the intersection of them all.

—*Kayla Parker*

POEMS AND PRAYERS

Prayers and Dreamings

With a bow to Ysaye Barnwell and Stephanie Kaza

Spirit within all, mysterious force giving shape to
    life, miraculous source and river of being,
help us to know who we are, to see our place in the
    history of the earth and in the family of things;
help us to see that we are part of all that ever was—
our grandmother's prayers and our grandfather's dreamings,
our mother's courage and our father's hope.

In our bones lies the calcium of antediluvian
    creatures,
in our veins courses the water of seas;
we are part of all that ever was,
born of this earth, riders upon a cosmic ocean;
we are not separate from nature, we are nature,
part of that same spirit that turned scales into
    feathers and birdsong into speech;
we live by the sun; we move by the stars . . .
we eat from the earth; we drink from the rain.

The italicized lines quote the works of Ysaye Barnwell and Stephanie Kaza,
respectively.

O great spirit, help us know who we are
and fill us with such love for this holy creation
and gratitude for this awesome gift we call living,
that we might claim our inheritance and live out
    our calling
to bless the world and each other with our care.
Amen

—Becky Edmiston-Lange

God Release Me By Your Power

God release me by your power
To be who I'm born to be,
From my agony, your outing
Making me alive and free.

No more subject to oppression
Of the norms that others brought;
Not deny or complying
Agonized, with tension fraught.

Let me face the world unfettered,
Knowing I am good as you,
Dancing on to greet the dawning
Of a world that's fresh and new.

—Andrew Pratt

The Way

I must live my own way,
Refusing all that binds.
I must know my own mind
Among all other minds.
I must do my own deeds,
And in whatever lands.
I will know my own hands
Among all other hands.

I must forsake the crowds,
And walk with lonely fools,
To seek for my own face
In bleak, deserted pools.
I must leave worn old roads,
To walk on hillside grass,
To follow my own feet
Out in the wilderness.

—*Kenneth L. Patton*

Quicken in Me a Sense of Humor

O God of gifts,
quicken in me a sense of humor
    bright enough to help me find my way
        in these tarnished times,
    fruitful enough to be made the wine of hope
        to warm the hearts of those I live with.

Make me glad to be one of a kind,
   yet one with a kind,
      called not to be more like others,
         but more of myself,
            a guerrilla of grace,
               that, in daring to be authentic,
                  I may become more of a human-kind.

So, O God of gifts,
liberate me to share,
   without apology or arrogance,
      not only the gifts I have,
         but the gift I am.

—Ted Loder

The Sun in Drag

You are the Sun in drag.
You are God hiding from yourself.
Remove all the "mine"—that is the veil.
Why ever worry about
Anything?
Listen to what your friend Hafiz
Knows for certain:
The appearance of this world
Is a Magi's brilliant trick, though its affairs are
Nothing into nothing.
You are a divine elephant with amnesia

Trying to live in an ant
Hole.
Sweetheart, O sweetheart
You are God in
Drag!

—*Hafiz*

When I Heard at the Close of the Day

When I heard at the close of the day how my name had been
    receiv'd with plaudits in the capitol, still it was not a happy
    night for me that follow'd,

And else when I carous'd, or when my plans were accomplish'd,
    still I was not happy,

But the day when I rose at dawn from the bed of perfect health,
    refresh'd, singing, inhaling the ripe breath of autumn,

When I saw the full moon in the west grow pale and disappear
    in the morning light,

When I wander'd alone over the beach, and undressing bathed,
    laughing with the cool waters, and saw the sun rise,

And when I thought how my dear friend my lover was on his
    way coming, O then I was happy,

O then each breath tasted sweeter, and all that day my food
    nourish'd me more, and the beautiful day pass'd well,

And the next came with equal joy, and with the next at evening
    came my friend,

And that night while all was still I heard the waters roll slowly
    continually up the shores,

I heard the hissing rustle of the liquid and sands as directed to
    me whispering to congratulate me,
For the one I love most lay sleeping by me under the same
    cover in the cool night,
In the stillness in the autumn moonbeams his face was inclined
    toward me,
And his arm lay lightly around my breast—and that night I
    was happy.

—*Walt Whitman*

Legal Alien

Bi-lingual, Bi-cultural,
able to slip from "How's life?"
to "*Mestán volviendo loca*,"
able to sit in a paneled office
drafting memos in smooth English,
able to order in fluent Spanish
at a Mexican restaurant,
American but hyphenated,
viewed by Anglos as perhaps exotic,
perhaps inferior, definitely different,
viewed by Mexicans as alien,
(their eyes say, "You may speak
Spanish but you're not like me")
an American to Mexicans
a Mexican to Americans
a handy token

sliding back and forth
between the fringes of both worlds
by smiling
by masking the discomfort
of being pre-judged
Bi-laterally.

—Pat Mora

Marginal Wisdom

They teach us to read in black and white.
Truth is this—the rest false.
You are whole—or broken.
Who you love is acceptable—or not.
Life tells its truth in many hues.
We are taught to think in either/or.
To believe the teachings of Jesus—OR Buddha.
To believe in human potential—OR a power beyond a single
    will.
I am broken OR I am powerful.

Life embraces multiple truths, speaks of *both*, and of *and*.
We are taught to see in absolutes.
Good versus evil.
Male versus female,
Old versus young,
Gay versus straight.

Let us see the fractions, the spectrum, the margins.
Let us open our hearts to the complexity of our worlds.
Let us make our lives sanctuaries, to nurture our many
   identities.

The day is coming when all will know
That the rainbow world is more gorgeous than monochrome,
That a river of identities can ebb and flow over the static,
   stubborn rocks in its course,
That the margins hold the center.

—*Leslie Takahashi Morris*

REFLECTION

Pulled Between Parts

Identity is one of those concepts I have tried desperately to push to the sidelines for most of *mi vida*. It was always too complicated, too painful, or too divisive. To put it simply, I am a bi-racial, white-passing, queer, socio-economically poor, agnostic Unitarian Universalist college junior at an elite liberal arts college, who was raised by a Caucasian single mother. Like all people, my identities are complex and multi-faceted.

My father was a Mexican immigrant. My mom is of European descent and was born and raised in Michigan. Due to my pale skin and *ojos azules*, no one ever suspects that I am of anything other than European descent. I can call myself *mexicano* without ever experiencing what it is like to be the other. I can speak *español* fluently and have been able to fully participate in the Latino communities in my hometown. But all of that seems not to matter much because I will never be called *wetback* or *spick*. I will never be told to go back to my own country or to just speak *inglés*. To others, I will always be perceived as another well-meaning white guy flouting his privilege. I will never be the other when it comes to race.

While I am constantly told that I cannot possibly be Mexican, I love the Mexican part of my heritage. There are few things more comforting than making *tamales* from scratch on a rainy day or eating a *pastel de tres leches con mi familia*. I went to many *quinceañeras* when I was younger, and I speak to my Mexican grandparents only in *español*. Yes, my narrative does not seem to follow that of the average Mexican-American in the United States, but I don't think that matters. I feel Mexican, and I also feel a deep connection to my Michigan roots.

My experience is becoming more common within the larger American identity narrative. Many of my peers have described feeling pulled between two or more parts of their heritage that make up their cultural identity. We feel uniquely attached to certain parts of our cultural heritage in different ways and for different reasons. My own racial and ethnic identities have pulled me particularly to the third Principle of Unitarian Universalism, "acceptance of one another and encouragement to spiritual growth." It is this faith commitment that has given others and myself the space to discuss the multiplicity of our identities and acknowledge the privileges enjoyed by white and white-passing people in American society. This faith has helped me to bridge the gap between my personal identities and the way I am perceived in the world, something I tried to ignore for most of my life.

—*Saul Ulloa*

CLOSING WORDS

Our task is to be who we are, in every way we
can be; our salvation proceeding in putting
ourselves back together after each tumble. . . .
We irridesce, shine, and radiate. We exclaim
and roar: we are.

—*Kenneth Patton*

If I am not for myself, who will be for me?
And if I am for myself alone, what am I?
And if not now, when?

—*Hillel the Elder*

Lost and Found

So just be quiet and sit down.
The reason is—you are drunk,
and this is the edge of the roof.

—Rumi

Let us reach the place of self, the place that is
    not alien to truth.
Let us wash over with peace and serenity, with
    fierce longing for light and heart; with living
    strength flowing in our veins,
bring ourselves into fearlessness and into trust.

—Ma. Theresa Gustilo Gallardo

REFLECTION

Losing My Religion

I somehow lost my chalice necklace on Commonwealth Avenue in Boston the same day I lost my marriage and my religion. I must have dropped it while I was walking down the street. It was a bad day.

Let me back up. I grew up Unitarian Universalist. I had a chalice necklace for a long time that I only sometimes wore. When I went to divinity school in 2009, I started to change so much that I didn't recognize myself. I began to feel that Unitarian Universalism lacked depth and symbolism, and I began to love Jesus with a passion. I prayed to a radically loving and forgiving God I had never believed in before because I had never needed God until then. I had just finished a hospital chaplaincy internship. I just knew that I was going to die soon because I was thirty-five and if I live until I'm seventy then I'm officially middle aged, and I only had a little bit of time left to *make a difference in this world*. What if Unitarian Universalism couldn't help me do that? My marriage was crumbling at the same time, and I was *coming unhinged*. It turns out it wasn't just my chalice necklace that was lost. So was my soul. And my dignity. Has this ever happened to you?

So I wandered up and down Commonwealth Avenue, wiping away boogers and sobbing like my seven-year-old sobs when I'm mad at her, looking for my chalice necklace and actually saying out loud over and over again, "What does it mean? What does it mean?"

I talked to my therapist and a mentor about this incident, asking them if it meant God wanted me to be a Christian and not a UU. They confirmed to me that yes, I was coming unhinged. My mentor gave me one of her extra chalice necklaces and made me some soup.

Two years later, my sanity restored, I finally purchased a new chalice necklace at General Assembly in the shape of a cross. I thought, "this is how I can honor the place I have come to in my spiritual journey . . . where Jesus and Unitarian Universalism hug on this cross." I wore it every day. People commented on it all the time. "I thought you were a UU. Why are you wearing a *cross*?" This made me feel very annoyed and, at the same time, gave me the kind of self-satisfied pride that comes from rebelling against your mom.

The week before my ordination, I returned home from church and realized that my chalice cross was missing from my neck. So I did what any totally sane thirty-something does. I took to Facebook to ask my Facebook friends, "*What does it mean?!*"

And my Facebook friends said a bunch of things, from "You need a better clasp on your chain" to "It means you don't need outward symbols to know what is in your heart." The most useful advice of all was: "Get a tattoo. You can't lose that."

The next day, I found my cross chalice, with its chain missing, in my inside coat pocket. So here's what gives me hope for the next time I am feeling off the chain: When I am lost, I will always be found. I will always be found by the Love that won't let me go. That Love doesn't exist only in symbol. Instead, it almost always comes in the form of people—talking sanity, making me soup, and telling me what it all means.

—*Robin Bartlett*

POEMS AND PRAYERS

Grounded

It hurts to let go of intensity
that zapped like electricity
yesterday.

It hurts to disconnect arcing power,
watch it ground and vanish.

What was it that surged through us
to lighten gray, indifferent skies?

What was it that connected
our hearts to hope?

Now we must wait,
for that inward current
to arc us forward again,
connecting our quest for justice
to the power of inner peace.

—*Stephen Shick*

Within the Light

Headlights, taillights, going, coming;
it does not matter inside.
Draw a curtain across the window,
lock the door and break the key.
Let the interior deepen and broaden
until it exceeds this little room.
You will go out when you are ready,
when the tiny inner Self no longer fits.
Awareness will come, yet bliss is not the goal:
pure consciousness, a word to the stranger
become friend, that is All.

—Jean M. Olson

To Bhain Campbell

I told a lie once in verse. I said
I said I said I said "The heart will mend,
Body will break and mend, the foam replace
For even the inconsolable his taken friend."
This is a lie. I had not been here then.

—John Berryman

The Way Out

In order to get out
I must go through.
      There is no other way.
No other way?
But there must be another way,
   an easier path, a well-lit road.
I cast about, scan the horizon—
   No other way.
      The way out is the way through.

The way through is the way hard.
Beset behind and before,
   a heavy hand laid upon me.
Pass one trial, meet another,
   leap one hurdle, run against another.
No turning back, no detours—
     no other way.

Lord, how long?
As long as it takes to get me there.
   Going down to go up,
   Approaching heaven via hell,
No other way.
     The only way out is through.

                —Kathy Fuson Hurt

Contact

I stretch forth my hand
    Knowing not what I shall touch . . .
        A tender spot,
        An open wound,
        Warmth,
        Pulsing life,
        Fragile blossoms,
        A rock,
        Ice.

I am tentative, trembling . . .
    Wishing to avoid hurt,
    Wanting to link my life with Life.
        Lonely, I desire companions
        Naked, I long for defenders.
        Lost, I want to find . . .
            to be found.
        Will I touch strangers
            Or enemies
            Or nothing?

My hand is withdrawn
    But still it touches
        My vulnerable skin, my furrowed brow,
        My empty pocket, my full heart.
        Do others reach, tremble, withdraw?
        Do they desire, long, seek?

Are they lonely, fearful, lost?
Will they grasp a tentative, trembling hand?

I stretch forth my hand
   Knowing not what I shall touch . . .
   But hoping . . .

                    —*Gordon B. McKeeman*

From the Shore

shouting back to Stevie Smith
who cried "I'm drowning! Not waving!"

I ain't waving babe, I'm drowning
going down in a cold lonely sea
I ain't waving babe, I'm drowning
so babe quit waving at me

I ain't waving babe, I'm crying
I'm crying, oh why can't you see?
I ain't fooling babe, I ain't fooling
so babe quit fooling with me

this ain't singing babe, it's screaming
I'm screaming that I'm gonna drown
and you're smiling babe, and you're waving
just like you don't hear a sound

I ain't waving babe, I'm drowning
going down right here in front of you
and you're waving babe, you keep waving
hey babe, are you drowning too?

—*Ric Masten*

Go Boldly

May you be brave enough to expose
your aching woundedness
and reveal your vulnerability.

May you speak your deepest truths,
knowing that they will change as you do.

May you sing the music within you,
composing your own melody,
playing your song with all your heart.

May you draw, paint, sculpt, and sew,
showing the world your vision.

May you write letters, poetry, biography,
slogans, graffiti, the great novel,
laying bare your words to love and hate.

May you love even though your heart
breaks again and again.

And until the end of your days,
may your life be filled
with possibilities and courage.

—*Jean M. Olson*

We Are Whole

We are whole,
even in the broken places,
even where it hurts.

We are whole,
even in the broken places,
the places where fear impedes our full engagement with life;
where self-doubt corrupts our self-love;
where shame makes our faces hot and our souls cold.

We are whole,
even in those places where perfectionism blunts the joy
of full immersion into person, place, activity;
where "good enough" does not reside except in our silent
    longings;
where our gaps must be fast-filled
with substance, accomplishment, or frenzied activity
lest they gape open and disgust.

We are whole
where we would doubt our own goodness, richness, fullness
    and depth,

where we would doubt our own significance, our own
profoundness.

We are whole,
even in our fragility;
even where we feel fragmented, alone, insubstantial, insufficient.

We are whole,
even as we are in process,
even as we stumble,
even as we pick ourselves up again,
for we are whole.

We are whole.

—Beth Lefever

REFLECTION

Found While Lost

"The beauty of the world is the mouth of a labyrinth," writes Simone Weil. We would be foolish not to follow its call. And so we enter the labyrinth, lured by the whiff of a dream still in the making: the possibility of a new relationship, the promise of a new career, the potential for a new beginning.

We can never be sure what we will find once inside. But this much is certain: there will be times when the beauty of the world, and with it the entrance to the labyrinth, unexpectedly disappear. Some relationships will disintegrate, some careers will dissatisfy, some beginnings will disappoint. Unable to find the labyrinth's opening, we often find ourselves in frantic search of an escape, fumbling for the next step, tiring ourselves out in the process. Disheartened, dispirited, we feel disoriented. We get lost.

The question is not whether we will get lost in life, but rather how we will move through it in faith. Will we dwell on everything that we have lost? Or will we focus instead on everything that we have yet to find?

As it happens, there is much that awaits us in our lostness. Much to be excavated examined, even exalted. In not yet knowing what will be, we are afforded the opportunity to appreciate what already is. The things hiding in plain sight. A frayed relationship, for example, may reveal our deeper needs. An unfulfilling career may motivate us to seek out a mentor. A misstart, or a misstep, may remind us of our own fragile humanity. It may claw open our hearts and sensitize us to the suffering of others.

When lost, perhaps the greatest question our faith asks of us is this: How will we be found? Once the time is ripe, the stars align, and the way begins to open, will we be ready to embrace the mystery anew? Will we choose to trust anew, to risk anew, to hope anew? Will we allow ourselves to yet again be drawn in, swept up, taken over by that magic that makes life worth living?

In the words of Simone Weil: "For if [we do] not lose courage, if [we go] on walking, it is absolutely certain that [we] will finally arrive at the center of the labyrinth. And there God is waiting. . . ."

—*Erik W. Martínez Resly*

CLOSING WORDS

Weary the path that does not challenge. Doubt
is an incentive to truth and patient inquiry
leadeth the way.

—*Hosea Ballou*

May the lessons of the dark time of the year,
deepen our roots,
ground our spirits,
and keep us true to our whole selves;
May we find rest, know joy, and broaden
our view.

—*Jude Geiger*

Spirit of Life

OPENING WORDS

The best form is to worship God in every form.
—*Neem Karoli Baba*

Truly the universe is full of light, and has been these thousands of years; yet, for all that, we could not dispense with the sunshine of tomorrow, whether as a realization or as an assuring prediction.

—*Horace Greeley*

REFLECTION

The Butterfly Effect

The delicate, flapping wings of a butterfly have the power to set molecules of air in motion, in turn moving more molecules of air—a tiny act that is eventually capable of affecting weather patterns on the other side of the planet. This notion comes from a concept within Chaos Theory called the Butterfly Effect. Simply, the Butterfly Effect refers to a phenomenon in our world in which a small change in one place can result in equal or greater changes elsewhere. This may seem crazy—a tiny butterfly changing global weather patterns? Not only is the Butterfly Effect a real scientific theory but it's also an intriguing philosophical idea. I say all this because the Butterfly Effect affects the way I live my life and the decisions that I make in a way that no ideas about God ever have.

I'm no meteorologist, nor am I well versed in entomology, but ever since learning about the Butterfly Effect, I have been attracted to it because it demonstrates an important principle that is often forgotten. Namely, each of our actions has effects that are more profound than we think. Interconnection is a major theme found in nearly all of the world's religious and philosophical traditions. The interconnectedness of our universe is also one of the most significant revelations of physics: All components of matter are interconnected, interrelated, and interdependent. As Unitarian Universalists, we affirm and promote our responsibility to remain aware of interconnection through our seventh Principle: respect for the interdependent web of all existence.

Attention to interconnectivity reminds me, despite the many sociopolitical forces that work to divide us from one another, that I'm never alone in this world. It reminds me that each decision or action I make has reactions, and that those reactions reverberate as waves moving back and forth across our globe. This compels me to live my life aware of the consequences of my daily actions, from the purchases I make to personal interactions with others. I certainly do not always succeed, but I try. My awareness of interconnectivity and efforts to work against the illusion of division remain my most significant spiritual practice.

This spiritual practice also gives me the ability to stand in awe of interconnection, in awe of the Butterfly Effect and the power that comes with it. On rare occasions, I am reminded to stop and appreciate the divinity of interconnectivity revealed before my very eyes. This to me is awe-inspiring. This to me is divine.

—*Dana Capasso*

POEMS AND PRAYERS

T'hillah

Barukh atah, Emeth!
Blest are you, o Truth.
Like the fabled Moses,
I too can never claim to have seen you
"face to face."
Too often, I've hung my own face on you
and pretended that I know something I do not.
Indeed, my most honest heart confesses
that at most,
I have only caught the briefest glimpse of you
at the very edge of my eye,
and only when I get out of my own way,
my own rush, my own fury.

I sense your cool shadow on me
when I grow hot from the tears
I've been holding back,
or when I notice the sadness or whimsy
hiding in the silent eyes of those around me.

I sense your closeness when I gaze
at a star suddenly unveiled by a toreador cloud,

or catch at an early yellowness
in the leaves of the oak.

It's then I feel a brush of wings nearby,
and realize that I am only a small part of it all.
Then I know that I am not the
great high power of the world,
but only a puff of breath hidden amid the
mighty blasts of the great whirlwind
called the universe.
Like a lacewing barely floating
on the tip of a small blade of green grass is my life
from beginning to end, a short footnote to
a vast essay of stars and space unbounded,
an essay neither signed nor finally symbolic.
And yet this truth, your truth,
is no sadness, but a joy,
no lack but a blessing,
like the sight of a child at play,
totally absorbed in the moment, and glad.
Blest are you, O Truth, who plays in this silence
like a child in the waves of an infinite sea.
Barukh atah, Emeth.

—*Mark Belletini*

Poem in a Time of Peril

Of course truth is hard.
It is a rock.
Yet I do not think it will fall upon me
And crush me.
I do not think they can hammer it to bits
And stone me.

Help me place the rock in the strong current
Of these rushing waters.
I must climb upon it.
I must know how truth feels.
When I plunge naked
Into the bright depth of these waters,
I must know how truth feels.
When I am swept by the cold fury of these waters,
I must know, with my whole being, how truth feels.
I shall remember how truth feels.

I praise the rock.
I praise the river.
I fear the drought
More than death by water.

—*Barbara Rohde*

Utterance of the Timeless Word

You bring yourself before the sacred,
before the holy,
before what is ultimate and bigger than your lone life
bigger than your worries
bigger than your money problems
bigger than the fight you had with your sister and your aches
     and pains
bigger, even, than your whole being, your self who is
  part of
  and trapped within
  and blessed with
a body that does what you want
and doesn't do what you want
and wants all the wrong things
and wants all the right things . . .

You stand at the edge of mystery,
at the edge of the deep,
with the light streaming at you,
and you can't hide anything—not even from yourself,
when you stand there like that,
and then . . . what?

Maybe you call your pastor and say,
  What is this?
  What am I looking at?
  What do I do?

And your pastor comes and stands at the edge with you
and looks over.
She can't hide anything either, she thinks,
not even the fact that she doesn't know the answer to your
        question,
and she wonders if you can tell.

She thinks of all the generations who've come there before you
and cast words out toward the source of that light,
wanting to name it.
Somehow, she thinks to herself, the names stayed tethered to
        the aging world and got old
while the light remains timeless and burns without dimming.

    Meanwhile,
the armful of worries you brought to the edge of mystery
have fluttered to your feet.
Unobscured by these, you shine back, light emanating unto
        light.
You, with your broken heart and your seeking,
you are the utterance of the timeless word.
The name of the Holy is pronounced
through your being.

—*Angela Herrera*

What God Is Like

I did not know what God is like
Until a friendly word
Came to me in an hour of need—
And it was God I heard.

I did not know what God is like
Until I heard love's feet
on errands of God's mercy
Go up and down life's street.

I did not know what God is like
Until I felt a hand
Clasp mine and lift me when alone
I had no strength to stand.

I think I know what God is like,
For I have seen the face
Of God's son looking at me
From all the human race.

—James Dillet Freeman

The Eternal

It is not old,
   Yet it comes through the wisdom of the ages.
It is not young,
   Yet it comes through the passion of innocence.
It is not revolutionary,
   Yet it comes proclaiming change.

It is not solitary,
    Yet it travels alone, seeking the open heart.
It is not lonely,
    Yet it seeks relationship.
It is not attached,
    Yet it connects everything.
It is the fresh return of the eternal,
    And it demands our response.

                                    —Stephen Shick

The Atheist Prays

I am praying again
and how does one pray
    when unsure if anything hears?

In the world I know as reliable and finite
    when time and matter cycle back and forth
    and I understand the answers to so many puzzles
there are moments when knowing is nothing
and I
    this accumulation of systems, histories
    repetitions falls from me—
    how does one who is sure there is nothing
    pray?
I
dark gathered around my eyes
sit in this room cluttered with my certainties

asking
my one unanswered question
holding myself perfectly still to listen
fixing my gaze
just here

wondering.

—*Barbara Pescan*

Of Course

Of course I want the truth,
but here's the rub:

Truth doesn't sit around
still as a rock,

it breathes and flows
and turns inside out.

Ever seen a lion in a cage?
He paces and glowers.

That must be how God feels
locked in our little religions.

Look how big the sky is,
the deep distances between stars.

Little speck, that's you;
laughable speck, that's me.

How could we contain The Truth,
all that overwhelming light?

Our truth is just a pinprick
in mystery's velvet curtain.

Even so, see how we struggle
to fix an eyeball to that—

peepshow's tiny window.

—*Janet Hutchinson*

Materializing

In what form did the spirit
appear to you today,
the blossom of a flower,
the tug of a child's hand,
the silent twinkling stars,
an old woman smiling at the bus stop,
a lover's gentle hug,
a presence so close to your soul
you could almost touch it,
words of truth formed
unbidden in your mind?

The holy disguised in so many ways,
may your senses open wide in recognition.

—*Jean M. Olson*

REFLECTION

Where God Is

The first time my heart felt broken, I went to church. When my mom died, I went to church. When I failed a class, I went to church. When I failed a friend, I went to church. When I felt like I'd failed at life, I went to church.

I didn't go asking for forgiveness. I didn't go asking for salvation.

I went to church—a Unitarian Universalist church—to be reminded, through hugs from friends, awkward interactions with strangers, and inspired messages from leaders, that no matter how down I feel, I still matter. I still have worth.

My God says, "Whoever you are, you are enough. Whomever you love, you are enough. Whatever your race or ethnicity, you are enough. Whatever your abilities, you are enough. Whatever your economic class, you are enough. Whatever your gender identity, you are enough. Whatever you do for a living, you are enough. If you don't have a job right now, you are enough. You are a human being, and so you are enough!"

My God says this when we come together, worship together, listen deeply to one another, and love one another. This, I believe, is the God of our faith.

My minister in college started the prayer with the same words every Sunday. I don't remember most of it; I do recall that he used the phrase *alone together*. We experience life through our own lenses, yet we don't have to go it alone.

I know too well that grieving the loss of a parent is a long, exhausting road. I also know that walking alongside a mourning friend can feel, somehow, even more taxing. Being there for others is plain hard. It can be tough to work up the courage to talk with a newcomer. Yet I believe that it is in those public spaces that God or the Spirit of Life truly resides.

It may go against prevailing American individualism to say that we need other people. We like to believe that we can do everything on our own. I believe that the human spirit truly comes alive when we are challenged, prodded, and uplifted in community.

In the days after my mom's death, I felt like hiding. Doing so would have been perfectly okay. I decided, though, to go to church. My friends went with me, and the community held me up, as well as my family. Being in community was harder than being alone—yet it was what I needed. I needed to sit in that sanctuary with my UU friends. I needed to sing those hymns and hear the voices of others.

We don't have to go to service every Sunday—yet I do think that we need to show up somewhere, to some community. I believe that living out our faith requires interaction beyond our own selves. I believe it calls for community. I believe that's where God is. Through covenant with others, we reach God, we know we are enough, and we are made better. We strengthen our souls and increase our capacity for love and understanding.

—Kenny Wiley

CLOSING WORDS

The sacred is present and available to us
wherever we look or are willing to find it. If
we remain open and expectant—watching out
of the corners of our eyes, keeping our ears
cocked, putting away all preconceived ideas—
our lives will emanate the sacred.

—Abhi Prakash Janamanchi

There is no pebble in the soil so obscure, no
flower in the field so tiny, no star in the sky so
distant, that it does not reveal to us as much of
God as it possesses.

—John Haynes Holmes

Justice and Creation

OPENING WORDS

We must not only preach but live by what
we had received as truth, or else renounce it
honestly as impracticable.

—Adin Ballou

And what does the LORD require of you?
To act justly and to love mercy
and to walk humbly with your God.

—Micah 6:8

REFLECTION

Re-Birth

At age twenty, I had the fortune of traveling the world. Through a study abroad program, I journeyed to awe-inspiring destinations like India, Cuba, and South Africa. In the process, I witnessed extreme poverty, global wealth, power disparity, and the effects of war and militarism—all while assured of my safety and physical comfort.

Throughout my voyage, I became aware of the bubble within which I had these cross-cultural experiences—and within which I made sense of my whole life. I experienced my travels as getting smacked in the face by my own privilege—and it stung. And yet, I tried to remain open, to allow myself to be changed. To question or let go of what I had known before. To submit myself to a transformative experience and to answer whatever call the world offered me, hoping I could really listen.

When I returned to the United States, I struggled with what felt like more than reverse culture shock. All around me—in my suburban home, in my congregation, and at my liberal arts college—I saw now that my "normal life" was buffered from much of the world's suffering. Everything seemed the same, yet forever different. In the first few weeks, I went through the motions: mechanically carrying out administrative tasks by day, numbing my mind with television by night. That lifestyle kept me functioning through my grief and fear. Grief for the life I'd led, but could no longer reconcile with what I now knew about the world. Fear that I would *not*, in fact, be changed but would instead resume my previous, ignorant patterns and assumptions. I felt a great sense of urgency, a frantic need to reconfigure my life in accordance with my values.

Soon after, my first UUA General Assembly brought me back to life. I'd long had a deep love for Unitarian Universalism. Because of it I had built many of my strongest, deepest friendships. I had been trained as a leader and claimed my voice—through preaching in the pulpit or singing favorite hymns in the pews. But that week, I connected in a new way with the Unitarian Universalist commitment to social justice—a commitment I now felt aching deep in my bones.

No longer alone—rather, literally surrounded by leaders and resources for justice-making—I began to lay a new path. Throughout the following decade, I devoted myself personally and professionally to social justice, returning again and again to my faith—not only as a movement for justice but as a sanctuary of spirit. Sometimes I needed connection with others. Other times, I needed a safe place to fall apart. More than once, my quest for justice left me weary, jaded, frustrated, and lost. Yet in the cradle of religious community, knowing that I am one among many building a better world, I have been birthed and re-birthed.

—Betty Jeanne Rueters-Ward

POEMS AND PRAYERS

Breathe Restlessness into Me

Thank you for all I forget are gifts,
   not rights.
Forgive me for all the grievances
   I remember too well.
Save me from the self-pity,
   the self-seeking,
      the fat-heartedness
     which is true poverty.
Guide me, if I'm willing
   (drive me if I'm not)
      into the hard ways of sacrifice
        which are just and loving.
Make me wide-eyed for beauty,
   and for my neighbor's need and goodness;
wide-willed for peace-making,
   and for the confronting power
      with the call to compassion;
wide-hearted for love
   and for the unloved,
      who are the hardest to touch
        and need it the most.
Dull the envy in me which criticizes
   and complains life into a thousand ugly bits.

Keep me honest and tender enough to heal,
   tough enough to be healed of my hypocrisies.
Match my appetite for privilege
   with the stomach for commitment.
Teach me the great cost of paying attention
   that, naked to the dazzle of your back as you pass,
      I may know I am always on holy ground.
Breathe into me the restlessness and courage
   to make something new,
      something saving,
         and something true
that I may understand what it is to rejoice.

—Ted Loder

In the midst of a world

In the midst of a world
marked by tragedy and beauty
there must be those
who bear witness
against unnecessary destruction
and who, with faith,
rise and lead
in freedom,
with grace and power.
There must be those who
speak honestly
and do not avoid seeing

what must be seen
of sorrow and outrage,
or tenderness,
and wonder.
There must be those whose
grief troubles the water
while their voices sing
and speak
refreshed worlds.
There must be those
whose exuberance
rises with lovely energy
that articulates
earth's joys.
There must be those who
are restless for
respectful and loving
companionship among human beings,
whose presence invites people
to be themselves without fear.
There must be those
who gather with the congregation
of remembrance and compassion
draw water from
old wells,
and walk the simple path
of love for neighbor.

And,
There must be communities of people
who seek to do justice
love kindness and walk humbly with God,
who call on the strength of
soul-force
to heal,
transform,
and bless life.
There must be
religious witness.

—*Rebecca Parker*

Only Begun

Spirit of Life and Love, dear God of all nations:
There is so much work to do.
We have only begun to imagine justice and mercy.

Help us hold fast to our vision of what can be.
May we see the hope in our history,
and find the courage and the voice
to work for that constant rebirth
of freedom and justice.
That is our dream.
Amen.

—*William Sinkford*

Here We Are

Here we are:
children at the Big Party,
having our moment in the sun,
our piece of the action,
till our bodies give way
and we are called home.

We're one big, not-always-happy family,
given life and breath by an eternal parent
we dearly long to know.
Now we have our one shot at it,
our one time to be a conscious part
of this ongoing cavalcade.

It's not a free and easy trip.
We have to live with pain as well as pleasure,
temptation as well as promise,
loneliness as well as love,
fear as well as hope.
We have to live inside a coat of skin,
wrapped up in drives difficult to control
and dreams difficult to achieve.

And though we are the guests of honor,
we don't get to set the time of the party or its place,
nor are we consulted about the guest list.

This is our time, and there really is just one question:

What are we going to do with it?

—John Corrado

Each of Us Is an Artist

Each of us is an artist
Whose task it is to shape life
Into some semblance of the pattern
We dream about. The molding
Is not of self alone, but of shared
Tomorrow and times we shall never see.
So let us be about our task.
The materials are very precious
   and perishable.

—Arthur Graham

Let Us Make This Earth a Heaven

Let us make this earth a heaven, right here, right now.
Who knows what existences death will bring?
Let us create a heaven here on earth
where love and truth and justice reign.
Let us welcome all at our Pearly Gates, our Freedom Table,
amid singing and great rejoicing,
black, white, yellow, red, and all our lovely colors,

straight, gay, transgendered, bisexual, and all the ways
of loving each other's bodies.
Blind, deaf, mute, healthy, sick, variously-abled,
Young, old, fat, thin, gentle, cranky, joyous, sorrowing.
Let no one feel excluded, let no one feel alone.
May the rich let loose their wealth to rain upon the poor.
May the poor share their riches with those too used to money.
May we come to venerate the Earth, our mother,
and tend her with wisdom and compassion.
May we make our earth an Eden, a paradise.
May no one wish to leave her.
May hate and warfare cease to clash in causes
too old and tired to name; religion, nationalism,
the false false god of gold, deep-rooted ethnic hatreds.
May these all disperse and wane, may we see each others' true
    selves.
May we all dwell together in peace and joy and understanding.
Let us make a heaven here on earth, before it is too late.
Let us make this earth a heaven, for each others' sake.

—*Tess Baumberger*

Creating Fire

Is the fire going out?
Not in your belly,
for you are still alive,
but in your soul,
that place

where dreams
fuel commitment

where longings
shape action

where meaning
flames purpose

where passion ignites
and rekindles
your life fire.

If your soul smolders
dream on
till you flame
like a chalice of hope.

—*Stephen Shick*

A Prayer for Unfinished Business

Dear great lathe of heaven,
O foundry of souls,
You churning, burning cosmos which has wrought
    me on the infinite loom of your celestial body.
Spinning stars and indifferent stones: hear my
    prayer.
Do not curse me to perish with all my dreams
    fulfilled.

Do not afflict me with a vision so narrow and a heart
    so small,
That all my greatest hopes could be accomplished
    within a single lifetime.
Rather, bless me with an unquiet spirit.
Anoint me with impertinent oils.
Grant me dreams so great and numerous,
That I might spend the fullness of my days to realize
    them,
And have ample remaining to leave to my inheritors.
Holy gyre that bore me and must one day take me
    home,
Allow me the mercy to depart this life with
    unfinished business.

—Kelly Weisman Asprooth-Jackson

REFLECTION

Death in the Subway

On August 14th, 2013, a man was killed by a New York City subway train. I know because my friends saw it happen. It was late at night when they got to the station; the platform almost empty. When they saw the man passed out across the tracks, they did everything they could safely do to save him. But the train was already pulling in, moving too fast to stop in time.

We rushed to the station to support our friends while they waited for the detective to take witness statements. I watched as police officers, MTA officials, and EMTs walked up and down the platform, planning out what to do next. Nobody moved with urgency; we were all too late to save this man.

The next day I poured over the Internet, searching for news of who he was. I had never met this man before. Yet through his death, I felt connected to his life. I had hoped to read how society would preserve his memory.

Instead, all I found was a short, impassive post from a relatively obscure media source: *A man died Thursday morning after a southbound 3 train hit him in the 116th Street station. . . . Regular train service resumed about two hours later.*

Perhaps his family did not want to announce his name to the public. Perhaps he no longer had a family. Perhaps he was never identified. We believe our society has come so far. Yet how many human lives get taken for granted, disappearing each day, practically unnoticed? How have we learned to devalue so many human lives?

Men, women, and children are raped, abused, and killed, all because someone believes they don't matter enough. People still do not have access to clean water, solely because their society labels them as unworthy. Millions of dollars are spent incarcerating individuals based solely on the neighborhood they live in. Thousands of people worldwide die of hunger each day, yet the United States alone wastes billions of pounds of good food each year.

We pay attention when we hear the aftermath. We pay attention to the statistics, the death toll. We pay attention when we already see the train. But by then, it's too late.

What if we did not wait until it was too late? What if we did not wait for destruction, suffering, and death before we took action? All around the world, there are people in need of support. What if we looked to create new possibilities in this world and stepped up to the responsibility? We are all leaders, powerful and courageous in our own ways.

Every single person on this earth matters. We all deserve to live; we all deserve to create the life we envision. I don't know who that man was. But I know he matters.

Take action for social change, however that looks for you. Offer to help someone, before they even think to ask for support. Tell someone how much you care about them, even when you think it is not necessary. Live each day to the fullest. Be grateful in knowing that *you matter*. We all deserve to have our stories told, long after we are gone. How do you want to be remembered?

—*Rebecca Chin*

CLOSING WORDS

You get up in the morning, you brush your teeth, and you help another human being.

—*Paul Eisemann*

Look at the facts of the world. You see a continual and progressive triumph of the right. I do not pretend to understand the moral universe; the arc is a long one, my eye reaches but little ways; I cannot calculate the curve and complete the figure by the experience of sight; I can divine it by conscience. And from what I see I am sure it bends towards justice.

—*Theodore Parker*

Hope and Praise

OPENING WORDS

love is the voice under all silences,
the hope which has no opposite in fear;
the strength so strong mere force is feebleness:
the truth more first than sun more last than star

—E. E. Cummings

Enough, I say, of big things and great things,
And extraordinary things, and ultimate things.
I celebrate the ordinary.
I lift my voice in praise.

—Richard S. Gilbert

REFLECTION

The Best Age Yet

Every year on her birthday, my mother joyously proclaims that the age she is now is the best one yet. This November, she threw her arms in the air with feigned relief and said, "Thank goodness I am no longer sixty-one. Sixty-two is the very best age yet, I can already feel it. No offense to you kids, but being young is hard."

My mother's joy is contagious, and I think I may have caught a chronic case of it. Indeed, I also feel that each year is the best one, not so much because a particular age falls onto some good or bad spot on the arch of time, but because each age I become is the age during which I get to be alive. Each new year is another year to live this life in this body on this earth with these people, and for this I celebrate.

And my mother is right. Being young is not easy. Especially this kind of in-between young where people 18–35 find themselves, where autonomy and stability don't seem to co-exist for long. We are transitory, growing, uncertain, and searching. We are also open, bold, and unyielding. We are able to live this way because we have each other.

We look to the future, realizing that most of us have many decades left on this uncertain journey. We look to the future with the knowledge that, for the first time in generations, we have less financial and material security than our parents. We look to the future and see a world grown ever more divided economically, politically, and socially. We look to the future and we celebrate. The young adults I know look into the face of climate change and find an opportunity for community and solidarity; we stare down constricting job markets and contemplate paradigm change. We find opportunities for mini-ministry in everyday acts of misunderstanding and micro-aggression.

I am grateful for this difficult, challenging, hectic, scary, uncertain time. This is a Holy time for me, because in it I learn to rely on community. I always say my mother gave me life twice. First when she gave birth to me, and then again when she raised me in the Unitarian Universalist faith. I was raised with a built-in family. I was raised in the loving arms of Unitarian Universalist youth and young adult culture. I sustain my joy by reaching out to that community during the hard times.

My mother is a wise woman: Being young isn't easy, but for me it is bathed in the love of a community that continually celebrates life with joy.

—*Julie Brock*

POEMS AND PRAYERS

The Stars Are Dancing

The stars are dancing tonight,
while the moon sits in her golden hammock,
swaying back and forth
to the rhythm of celestial voices.

The Beloved is full of rapture,
dancing worlds and stars into being,
drunk with the wine of passion
and filling the heavens with song.

Do not sit alone in the dark
while creation sings three-part harmony.
Dance, my friends.
Dance wildly,
sing joyfully,
fill your heart with the beauty of the Beloved
as the Beloved turns your soul to light.

—*Om Prakash*

O Mystery!

O mystery beyond my understanding,
Voice in my heart answering to the earth
And light of distant stars!
O wonder of the spring, leading the seasons on:
The dewdrops sparkling on the web at sunrise,
And unseen life, moving in depths and shallows of the brook,
Trembling in raindrops at the edge of eaves,
Whisper to me of secrets I would know.
O power that flows through me and all that is,
Light of stars, pulsating in the atoms in my heart,
Whether you are mind and spirit
Or energy transcending human thought

I cannot know, and yet I feel
That out of pain and sorrow and the toil
Through which creation springs from human hands
A force works toward the victory of life, even through the stars.
Here on the earth winter yields slowly, strikes again, and hard,
And lovely buds, advance guards of the spring, suffer harsh death,
And pity moves the heart.
Yet life keeps pulsing on.
The stars still shine, the sun rises again,
New buds burst forth, and life still presses on.
O mystery!
I lift my eyes in wonder and in awe!

—*Robert T. Weston*

In Heaven

Ah, it's true.
When our ancestors spoke of heaven,
they were speaking of this moment.
When they went on about nirvana
they imagined a time like this.
When they sang of paradise,
it was this morning they imagined.
A time when all the mysteries of life and death
are blended in a community of praise,
when the bones of ancient lovers
are given flesh again in our own bodies,
teachers of long ago speaking of love and truth

once more in lives so ordinary they are
extraordinary.
Blest is our breath, in and out, quiet,
blest is our sitting, our fidgeting, our movement,
blest is our heartbeat echoing
the pounding alleluias of the distant stars,
blest is the silence that is presence,
not absence.

—Mark Belletini

We Must Be Saved

Nothing worth doing is completed in our lifetime;
Therefore, we are saved by hope.

Nothing true or beautiful or good makes complete sense
in any immediate context of history;
Therefore, we are saved by faith.

Nothing we do, however virtuous,
can be accomplished alone;
Therefore, we are saved by love.

No virtuous act is quite as virtuous
from the standpoint of our friend or foe as from our own;
Therefore, we are saved by the final form of love
which is forgiveness.

—Reinhold Neibuhr

Web

Intricate and untraceable
weaving and interweaving,
dark strand with light:

Designed, beyond
All spiderly contrivance,
To link, not to entrap:

Elation, grief, joy, contrition, entwined;
shaking, changing, forever forming, transforming;

All praise, all praise to the great web.

—*Denise Levertov*

The Way Things Work

is by admitting
or opening away.
This is the simplest form
of current: Blue
moving through blue;
blue through purple;
the objects of desire
opening upon themselves
without us;
the objects of faith.
The way things work

is by solution,
resistance lessened or
increased and taken
advantage of.
The way things work
is that we finally believe
they are there,
common and able
to illustrate themselves.
Wheel, kinetic flow,
rising and falling water,
ingots, levers and keys,
I believe in you,
cylinder lock, pully,
lifting tackle and
Crane lift your small head—
I believe in you—
your head is the horizon to
my hand. I believe
forever in the hooks.
The way things work
is that eventually
something catches.

    —*Jorie Graham*

"Hope" is the thing with feathers

"Hope" is the thing with feathers –
That perches in the soul –
And sings the tune without the words –
And never stops – at all –

And sweetest – in the Gale – is heard –
And sore must be the storm –
That could abash the little Bird
That kept so many warm –

I've heard it in the chillest land –
And on the strangest Sea –
Yet – never – in Extremity,
It asked a crumb – of me.

—Emily Dickinson

I Praise You for What Is Yet to Be

Wondrous Worker of Wonders,
I praise you, not alone for what has been,
   or for what is,
     but for what is yet to be,
for you are gracious beyond all telling of it.

I praise you
that out of the turbulence of my life
   a kingdom is coming,

is being shaped even now
    out of my slivers of loving,
        my bits of trusting,
        my sprigs of hoping,
        my tootles of laughing,
        my drips of crying,
        my smidgens of worshiping;
that out of my songs and struggles,
  out of my griefs and triumphs,
    I am gathered up and saved,
for you are gracious beyond all telling of it.

I praise you
that you turn me loose
  to go with you to the edge of now and maybe,
    to welcome the new,
      to see my possibilities,
        to accept my limits,
and yet begin living to the limit
  of passion and compassion
    until, released by joy,
      I uncurl to other people
        and to your kingdom coming,
for you are gracious beyond all telling of it.

—Ted Loder

REFLECTION

The 99%

"Look, look!" The strangers around me were shouting and pointing. I spun around. From my position halfway across the Brooklyn Bridge, I could see a large circle of light on the Verizon building, prominent in the New York City skyline. Inside the circle were three symbols that would have meant very little just three months earlier. But on that day, November 17, 2011, they were a beacon of hope and a cause for celebration, two nines and a percentage sign.

"We! Are! The ninety-nine percent!" We shouted in time to the flashing symbols as we took part in our protest march, delighting in this surprise subversion of corporate space. We laughed and cheered as the messages changed, scrolling through favorite chants. Finally the display reached its conclusion: Happy Birthday Occupy Wall Street! The social movement that had started with a motley crew of activists camping out in Zuccotti Park turned two months old that day.

The dose of joy was sorely needed. Two days earlier, I awoke to frantic messages on my phone. The police had arrived in the middle of the night and torn down the tent city I had come to love during my shifts with Protest Chaplains–NYC. I rushed down. The tents, kitchen, and library, the diverse and passionate crowds, were gone, revealing bare concrete guarded by police.

So we carried visceral anger and fresh sadness with us as we marched on November 17. Still, we celebrated. We celebrated because we knew we had already changed the world. The Occupy movement had shifted the national conversation about economic and political issues. We had encouraged folks to come together and live into their values in radical ways. So we celebrated our victories in the face of recent heartbreak and defeat.

We knew the road ahead would be rough. When Zuccotti was raided, the occupiers had become homeless. Still, we hoped. Our hope that night was not rooted in optimism for the future but in the reality of our powerful gathering. It grew from the certainty that we were standing on the side of love that night as we marched. It was nourished by the sense of connection we felt as we danced and sang and hooted with joy, the loving interconnection that sustains all life, that which I call God.

We must dare to hope and celebrate in that manner. We have faced disappointments and instances of defeat. We have seen the brokenness in individuals and social systems. And yet, we must celebrate. We must celebrate who we are and how we are changing lives, communities, laws, and society for the better.

When we celebrate our highest values and find that sacred hope within us, we are spiritually energized and driven in divine directions. We are moved toward one another, into loving interconnection, into deeper relationship with all that is holy.

—*Annie Gonzalez*

CLOSING WORDS

We must accept finite disappointment, but never
lose infinite hope.

—Martin Luther King Jr.

Be revered
In thee the faithful hope that still looks forward,
And keeps the life-spark warm of future action
Beneath the cloak of patient sufferance.

—Margaret Fuller

Hymns and Songs

Spirit of Life

Words and music by Carolyn McDade

Come, Come, Whoever You Are

Words: adapted from Jalaluddin Rumi
Music: Lynn Adair Ungar, © 1989 Lynn Adair Ungar

Gathered Here

Gath - ered here   in   the   mys-t'ry of the hour.

Gath - ered here   in   one   strong bod - y.

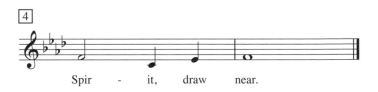

Gath - ered here   in   the   strug-gle and the pow'r.

Spir   -   it,   draw   near.

Words and music: Philip A. Porter, 1953– , © 1991 Philip A. Porter

Where Do We Come From?

3-part round
Words: Paul Gaugin and Brian Tate, © 1999 Brian Tate
Music: Brian Tate, © 1999 Brian Tate

Meditation on Breathing

Words and music: Sarah Dan Jones, © 2001 Sarah Dan Jones

Building Bridges Between Our Divisions

1 ♩=96

Build - ing bridg-es be - tween our di - vi-sions, I

2

reach out to you, will you reach out to me? With

3

all of our voic-es and all of our vi-sions,

4

friends, we could make such sweet har - mo - ny.

Words: The women of Greenham Common peace occupation in England, 1983
Music: Contemporary English Quaker Round

Blue Boat Home

Fluid, legato ♩=140

1. Though be - low me, I feel no mo - tion stand - ing on these moun - tains and plains. Far a - way from the roll - ing o - cean still my dry land heart can say: I've been sail - ing

2. Sun my sail and moon my rud - der as I ply the star - ry sea, lean - ing o - ver the edge in won - der, cast - ing ques - tions in - to the deep. Drift - ing here with my

3. I give thanks to the waves up - hold - ing me, hail the great winds urg - ing me on, greet the in - fi - nite sea be - fore me, sing the sky my sail - or's song: I was born up -

Words: Peter Mayer, 1963– , © 2002 Peter Mayer
Music: Roland Hugh Prichard, 1811–1887, adapted by Peter Mayer, © 2002 Peter Mayer

all   my   life___ now,   nev - er
ship's   com - pan - ions,   all we
on   the   fath - oms,   nev - er

har - bor or   port have I known.   The
kin - dred pil - grim souls,
har - bor or   port have I known.   The

wide   u - ni - verse___   is   the o -
mak - ing our way___ by the lights_
wide   u - ni - verse___   is   the o -

- cean I   trav - el___
___ of   the heav - ens___
- cean I   trav - el,___

and the earth___ is my___ blue
in our beau - ti - ful___ blue
and the earth___ is my___ blue

boat   home.___
boat   home.___
boat   home.___

Rise Up O Flame

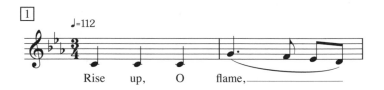

Rise up, O flame,

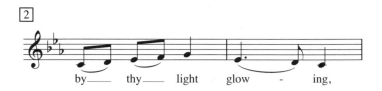

by thy light glow - ing,

show to us beau - ty,

vi - sion, and joy.

Words: Anonymous
Music: Christoph Praetorius

One More Step

1. One more step, we will take one more step, 'til there is peace for us and ev - ery - one, we'll take one more step.
2. One more word, we will say one more word, 'til ev - ery word is heard by ev - ery - one, we'll say one more word.
3. One more prayer, we will say one more prayer, 'til ev - ery prayer is shared by ev - ery - one, we'll say one more prayer.
4. One more song, we will sing one more song, 'til ev - ery song is sung by ev - ery - one, we'll sing one more song.

Words and music: Joyce Poley, © 1986 Joyce Poley

I Know This Rose Will Open

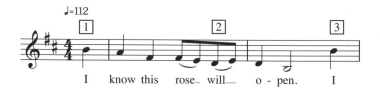

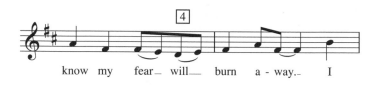

I know this rose will o-pen. I

know my fear will burn a-way. I

know my soul will un-furl its wings. I

know this rose will o - pen.

Words and music: Mary E. Grigolia, 1947– , © 1989 Mary E. Grigolia

Guide My Feet

Words and music: Traditional

Go Now in Peace

Go   now in peace.   Go   now in peace.

May   the   love   of   God   sur - round   you

ev - ery - where,   ev - ery - where

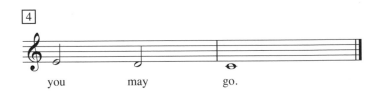

you   may   go.

Words and music: Natalie Sleeth, 1930– , based on Luke 2:29, © 1976 Hinshaw Music, Inc.

UNITARIAN
UNIVERSALIST

About Unitarian Universalism

Whether you are engaging with this faith for the first time or the billionth: Welcome home. Throughout these pages, may you feel an invitation to journey through life with these Unitarian Universalist young adults and our many varied sources. And may you feel the invitation again and again, throughout life.

Unitarian Universalists are thinkers and doers. We have different beliefs, backgrounds, ethnicities, and spiritual practices. We unite in creating justice and love, and in countering oppression and hate.

How to find a Unitarian Universalist community near you:

- Find a congregation by visiting **uua.org** and entering your information in the "find a congregation" box.
- Find a young adult or campus ministry group near you by visiting the UU Young Adult "Hub" on Facebook (**facebook.com/HubYAUU**).
- Find what else can be found by contacting the young adult ministries within the Office of Lifespan Faith Engagement at **youngadults@uua.org** or visiting **uua.org/youngadults**.

Principles

Unitarian Universalism affirms and promotes seven Principles:

1. The inherent worth and dignity of every person
2. Justice, equity, and compassion in human relations
3. Acceptance of one another and encouragement to spiritual growth in our congregations
4. A free and responsible search for truth and meaning
5. The right of conscience and the use of the democratic process within our congregations and in society at large
6. The goal of world community with peace, liberty, and justice for all
7. Respect for the interdependent web of all existence of which we are a part.

Sources

Unitarian Universalism draws from many Sources:

1. Direct experience of that transcending mystery and wonder, affirmed in all cultures, which moves us to a renewal of the spirit and an openness to the forces which create and uphold life;
2. Words and deeds of prophetic people which challenge us to confront powers and structures of evil with justice, compassion, and the transforming power of love;
3. Wisdom from the world's religions which inspires us in our ethical and spiritual life;
4. Jewish and Christian teachings which call us to respond to God's love by loving our neighbors as ourselves;
5. Humanist teachings which counsel us to heed the guidance of reason and the results of science, and warn us against idolatries of the mind and spirit;
6. Spiritual teachings of Earth-centered traditions which celebrate the sacred circle of life and instruct us to live in harmony with the rhythms of nature

History

Drawn from many Sources and grounded in shared Principles, Unitarian Universalism has its roots in liberal Christianity. In 1961, the separate Unitarian and Universalist denominations consolidated to create the Unitarian Universalist Association, declaring their sources and beliefs were no longer only Christian. Today, we are a theologically diverse group of believers who discover and grow together in community.

UUA Office of Lifespan Faith Engagement

The mission of the Office of Lifespan Faith Engagement: Co-Creating a Transformative Faith. . . . We put a justice seeking, radically inclusive faith in action by:

- creating experiences for meaning-making and faithful living
- accompanying people to make a home in our faith
- advocating for youth engagement and lifespan faith development

To accomplish this we connect leaders, equip congregations, and engage youth and young adults in promoting dynamic, multicultural, and multigenerational ministry, leadership development, connection, and support for people of all ages engaged in UU youth and young adult ministry. The Office's primary programs include:

- exploration of new forms of faithful community and spiritual development
- regular social media presence and online communication, including Blue Boat, a blog of youth and young adult ministries
- campus ministry support and coordination
- tools, materials, and resources for youth and young adults engaged in ministry in their own communities
- coordination and collaboration with other UUA offices, committees, and related groups
- grants, awards, and recognition for outstanding youth and young adult ministry
- programs for youth and for young adults at the Association's annual General Assembly

The Office can be reached at youngadults@uua.org or 617-948-4350, or visit us online at **uua.org/youngadults**

We gratefully acknowledge permission for the following: